KNOWLEDGE WINS

Creating Knowledge for Competitive Advantage

and

Managing Success

By

Tim Walters

ISBN 978-1-105-72314-8
90000

9 781105 723148

TABLE OF CONTENTS

List of Figures

<u>Preface</u>

The business world of today is rapidly changing. These changes are being brought about by various factors. A global economy, technological advancements, and changing world demographics are just three of the many issues modern organizations must face. Additionally, the business environment varies dramatically around the world. Business law, taxes, and regulations; create a variety of environment's; Even cultural norms have significant impact on the organization.

In order to deal with the continuously changing environment, businesses must continually create and re-evaluate the policies and structure, which guide the organization.

I propose the most important ingredient to competitive

success is the quality of the human resources of the organization. The ability to learn, retain, and utilize knowledge is the reason the human resource is so valuable. Additionally, this work promotes the following idea. While the characteristics of the individual employees make the difference between success and failure for the entire organization, the characteristics of the management is of greater importance. In order to create "knowledge workers", organizations need "knowledge managers".

ONE

Introduction

By the time this sentence is read, approximately a dozen new infants will have taken their first breath somewhere in the world. Each day there are about 200,000 individuals added to the population of the planet, and it is estimated that the world population is growing by approximately 73,000,000 people per year.

All of these people have a dramatic affect on the world they live in. People cause change. People create products, they come up with new ideas, and they compete for resources. Technology is a product of human hands, and technology feeds off itself. The result is more people create more innovation, and

1

more innovation exponentially leads to greater technological advancements.

Think for a moment, about the world you knew as a youth, what has changed? When I was growing up the world did not know of the Internet. Microsoft was not yet a corporation. Phones were something in your home and were still owned by the phone company. While knowledge was readily available in such places as the university or the library, it was certainly not available in your pocket, with the speed equivalent of 100 telephone lines combined. Via your wireless smartphone; today, we can access the world- wide web and all of its possibilities from almost anywhere in seconds.

More people, more technology, more information, more processing power, and more access to all of these results in an environment that is rapidly changing. Combine this with the global economy and a myriad of other issues; and the modern organization confronts continuous change. The question then arises, how can businesses function and effectively compete in such a volatile environment?

Clearly, there is no single right answer to this question. Many organizations with different structures, processes, and management styles and practice are successful in today's current environment. In the future, it can be expected some of the same organizations, as well as, many new organizations will also be successful.

While success can be achieved through various means, successful organizations likely exude some similar characteristics. One such characteristic is the knowledge of the firm. There is a reason Microsoft was created by Bill Gates and not IBM; Mr. Gates obviously was knowledgeable enough too recognized and act on the opportunity and value that IBM did not, in the early development of the Microsoft solutions. The knowledge of the firm can take many forms. It can be knowledge of the business, the product or service, the environment, or anything else related to the concepts, processes, organization, or market. Because knowledge of the business, environment, or market leads to success; the greater is the knowledge of the organization, the greater is the likelihood of competitive success.

To illustrate the importance of knowledge to competitive success, take the example of how knowledge flows through an organization. The existence of the operation relies on the ability to generate or create the marketable idea, communicate the information through the organization in such a way to allow the value to be transferred, utilized, and implemented effectively, in order to exploit the asset of the knowledge. This concept applies to businesses of any size, whether it is a small business or a large

3

corporation, whether it relies on a single individual to originate new ideas, services, or product offerings; or whether it has an entire organization dedicated to the task. Knowledge, its transfer, and application are crucial to success.

Knowledge assets are the basis of an individual's or an organization's product or service offerings. As an engineer working on wireless communication networks, I often like to joke about "exploiting a principle of science for monetary gain". I think of it as a funny way to describe my work, but dig deeper and realize the following: radio waves travel through space (a principle of science), phone companies acquire licenses for available spectrum and transmit radio waves in a coordinated way (application of knowledge), to make profits (improved competitive success). Wireless companies do not make possible the physics of radio waves, they merely recognize and act on the opportunity, based on the knowledge. The ability to actualize value from one's vision and capability, to seize and capitalize on opportunity, and to continually modify capabilities through continuous evaluation and improvement all represent dynamic capabilities and knowledge which directly impacts success.

Knowledge is the most important strategic resource for competitive advantage: having superior intellectual resources allows organizations to "do more with less". Even in cases where

4

the science, raw materials, etc. level the competitive landscape, the more knowledgeable business or workforce will gain competitive advantage by acquiring new knowledge, integrating, sharing, and applying the assets to build and sustain advantage.

If firms accept the premise that possessing organizational knowledge is important to competitive success, then it is logical that firms should attempt to acquire knowledge. Before this can be done however, that knowledge should be defined and where it resides identified.

Knowledge can be defined as facts, truths, or principles about "things". Facts as an example, can be located, identified, researched, and empirically tested. In this way knowledge seems to be an object which can be recognized, measured, and acquired. But knowledge is more than just an object; it is one thing to have knowledge in your possession, it is quite another to understand it and know how to apply it. The act of knowing represents the familiarity or experience with the "object" knowledge. It is this experience which allows for knowledge to be applied, developed, and managed.

To know something is inherently human. While knowledge can be virtually anything, knowledge itself resides in individuals. Thus it is the individual, who has the greatest impact on the knowledge of the firm and by direct correlation, success.

The significance of the individual to organizational knowledge, and therefore competitive success, has resulted in the rise of the term "knowledge worker". This label has been used to describe these important individuals who possess the knowledge and ability to noticeably improve the competitive success of an organization, regardless of the environment.

Returning to the original question, how can businesses function and compete in today's volatile environment? Just as people are one of the largest sources of change, people, more specifically "knowledge workers", are fundamental to the competitive success of the modern organization. There are several methods by which firms can attain this crucial resource. Companies can simply hope to be fortunate enough to access knowledge workers through the new hire process. Businesses can attempt to acquire knowledge workers by attracting them from competitors. Alternatively, they can actively work to create and develop their own knowledge workers, specific to their needs, to improve competitive success.

The Proposition

It is unrealistic to believe significant numbers of knowledge workers will miraculously appear, on their own, in the organization and positions necessary. Organizations can seek out existing knowledge workers currently employed elsewhere; however, getting these individuals to hire-on can often be difficult and require paying a premium beyond what the current employer paid. Additionally, the knowledge possessed by these individuals is often specific to the organization or position and will likely require some modification. Alternatively, the typical hiring process will also provide some number of employees, who will naturally develop and exude characteristics of knowledge workers.

I propose the most effective means of obtaining knowledge workers is for the firm to create or develop their own workers and organization specific knowledge. I will present several characteristics of people which lead to organizational success and improved competitiveness. I will present the elements which allow organizations to develop knowledge workers. Lastly, I will focus on the importance of management to the development of the individual.

TWO

Issues Facing Business

In order to understand the importance of people to organizational success and to better understand how human resources can improve the likelihood of organizational success, one should be aware of the issues organizations face. While there are a wide range of issues and changes which could be detailed, I would like to focus on three specific areas of interest: people, technology, and environment.

A technology based aspect of change in the current workplace is the advent of "the virtual organization" with distributed, electronically linked workers. The virtual organization has replaced the office-centric workforce of yesterday. Several factors are leading to the virtual organization;

the rapid evolution of electronic technologies, and the continuous development of digital, wireless, audio, video, and data applications allow people to work with almost anyone from virtually anywhere. The rapid growth and application of the Internet, computer usage, and network capabilities, and the growth of telecommuting, the mobile office, and the home office have resulted in a shrinking world where people use technology to form organizations over great distance.

These new organizations are far removed from the historical counterpart, represented by the office manager, with direct reports, in a local office. This rapid technological change requires individuals capable of assimilating the technology and utilizing the technology in a changing environment. To emphasis this point, try to make a mental list of the number of computer applications you use on a typical day at work. You have been using many of them for some time and have developed a level of expertise. Imagine if you had never used any of them: what would it take for you learn them all from scratch today.

A second technology related change is the increased utilization of computerized performance monitoring and coaching tools. By automating coaching, training, and performance feedback, employee dependence on management will decrease and self-directed learning will increase. Self-motivated individuals whom are willing and eager to learn will be most desirable, and the more these employees learn, the more knowledgeable and desirable they become, and the greater they can contribute to organizational success.

A third challenge is the arrival of the "Just-in Time" workforce. Just in time manufacturing has been in use for some time to reduce operation costs and improve profitability. Similar concepts can be applied to workers. As companies reduce operations, using contractors, vendors, and temporary workers; outsourcing typically is associated to reducing costs. This activity can have impact on numerous issues from motivation and training to coaching and compensation. An example would be as fewer people are required to perform more roles, full-time employees may be performing the aspects of the job which are more detailed or require more knowledge, while facilitating temporary workers to perform the repetitive or menial functions. Alternatively over worked employees can be overstressed and under-performing. Motivation, training, coaching, and compensation would be different for each of these types of employees.

Another issue challenging businesses today is the topic of this book, the ascendancy of knowledge workers. Possessing a greater technical ability and often time's greater knowledge of past successes and failures makes these employees more productive. Yet, knowledge workers also present issues in the form of motivation, coaching, and compensation.

Additional workplace issues are presented by the growth of worker diversity and the aging of the workforce. These social aspects of the organization have obvious impacts which can lead to social issues in the workplace.

Combining the previously mentioned issues, we can clearly see a dynamic workforce takes shape. Work is no longer just a job, but a fluid environment that requires workers to continuously adapt. Employees must do what needs to be done and not just what was listed on a job description. Continuous improvement is needed to meet customer requirements and competitor actions, and professionals need to effectively utilize technology and adapt quickly to changing environments.

The issues faced by organizations today can be categorized into three areas: people issues, technology issues, and environmental issues. The virtual workforce and use of computerized performance monitoring are the result of changes in technology. The just in time workforce and the dynamic workforce are the result of changes in the workplace or business environment. People issues are evident in the aging workforce, employee diversity, and the rise of the knowledge worker.

Because people, technology, and the environment present formidable issues, the effective management of people, technology, and the environment will have a dramatic affect on how well organizations compete and survive.

In 1850, the World population was approximately 1.1 billion. Over the next 150 years, the population grew six fold to approximately 6 billion. It is estimated that fully one third of the current population is less than 15 years of age. The result of the natural increase is more and more people are exposed to increasing opportunities for learning, that which is known is changing rapidly, and the "impossible" is being performed every day. The demographics of the workforce are also changing. Changing ethnic population growth rates and the aging Baby Boomer generation has an impact on worker diversity.

Increased diversity in post secondary education and increasing levels of highly educated immigrants coming to the United States results in a dynamically changing workforce. In the new economy, processing information is often more powerful than processing products and the value of a company is to be found in people and ideas more than in operations.

While people provide opportunity, they also provide challenges. People issues such as turnover and employee productivity have a direct impact on the financial health of an organization. Employee ideas, feelings, attitudes, motivation, training, relationships, values, and various other human concerns all must be managed effectively to improve organizational success.

Technology must also be managed effectively to improve organizational success. As a result of technological advances, space and time have changed. In a shrinking world, distance is becoming meaningless and timeframes have collapsed. No longer is geography the major determinant of who competes with whom. The whole world is the customer and the competitor. Businesses connect instantly with customers all over the globe, requiring a faster time to market and ever-shorter response times.

Technology can change existing industries and contribute to the creation of new industries, rapidly changing the business landscape. Technology and innovation boost productivity and increase efficiency. This in turn changes the existing relationships and competitive success of individual businesses. The shrinking half-life of technical skills continually requires competitors to upgrade skills or fall behind, and the ability of investment, education, and training to keep up with technological innovation has become an important element of competitive success.

Technological change and the influence of more diverse people come together to form today's business environment. Today's products and services are bigger, faster, smarter, and cheaper. Productivity and efficiency are increasing. Computer networks are growing. Increasingly, information overload is becoming a problem. In order to make the most of greater amounts of information, capable employees are needed to master the technology and tools.

The proliferation of the Internet, electronically linked people and networks, and network based business information speeds up the decision process. The faster decision making ability requires faster decisions. Shortened response time leaves fewer gaps in the system and more JIT decision making. All of which again changes the nature of the competitive balance. The environment is continually subject to more change and more stress which has a direct impact on the workplace.

The workplace itself is starting to change; a distributed workforce and mobile employees are changing the nature of communications and coordination of work activities. The advent of home, mobile, and globally distributed offices can bring the organization closer to the customer and allow the employee the ability to meet personal needs, but they also change the working environment and the nature of the relationships employees develop, as well as the ability to develop them.

The marketplace has become global. This presents greater opportunity and with it higher risk. There exist more markets and opportunity, but more competition provides more incentive to innovate and cut costs. Additionally, issues like free trade and open financial systems change the competitive landscape.

The greater opportunity presented by today's environment also impacts the activities of employees. Greater opportunity and mobility has resulted in more employee turnover. Changing jobs for advancement or preference, job jumping, and overall attitudes toward employment are all changing. While some of this activity has slowed during the recent economic crisis, this condition is not likely to continue to be the norm.

Changing worldwide economic conditions and the changing economic environments of various countries can have an impact on the competitiveness of businesses operating within these markets. Closing the technology gaps between nations can change the environment rapidly.

People, technology, and the environment present challenges to organizational success. The management of people, technology, and the environment directly impacts nearly all aspects of business. Business models, economies of scale, the supply chain, inventory, and operating costs, to name a few, are directly linked to the management of these three issues. Businesses that master the management of these issues will have greater profits and greater market share. Managed poorly, these challenges will result in employee turnover, lost revenue, lost productivity, and major dislocations and uncertainty for workers and businesses.

THREE

People are a Key to Success

While the issues facing business are formidable,
individuals can possess characteristics, which allow them to
effectively deal with the challenges. There are several
characteristics which seem to be present in the employees of
successful organizations. These characteristics are innately
human and can only be found in individuals; and because these
characteristics are important to organizational success, people
who possess these traits are also important to organizational
success.

The first characteristic is competency and the ability to
continuously learn. This is the most important value which
people bring to an organization. If this characteristic could be

19

listed on a corporate balance sheet it would be defined as intellectual capital: material in the form of knowledge that has been defined and leveraged to produce a higher-valued output. The skill with which information is manipulated and applied is a key factor in the competitiveness of businesses.

In order to remain competitive, it is becoming more important for organizations to employ knowledgeable workers. Well-educated, well-trained, and highly skilled human resources are better prepared to meet the needs of a changing environment and contribute to organizational success.

An example that supports the importance of individual competency is the fact that companies develop policies and processes to increase employee competency. A competency building process can assist individuals in developing the characteristic of competency. Such a process can link people with existing knowledge and leverage diverse resources that exist within the organization. The results created by this process can then improve the likelihood of organizational success. The competency building process is one of the key processes of successful organizations.

Possessing competency and the ability to continually learn and increase knowledge is extremely vital in today's business environment. When people with this characteristic are attracted to a company, chances of success, competitiveness, and responsiveness to the changing environment are all improved.

The second characteristic of people, which makes them key to organizational success, is self-initiative. It is my opinion, in the history of man, few good things just happen. Did the United States and all it represents in terms of freedom of man, just happen, or was it possibly the result of the vision and desire of the founding fathers? In the majority of cases, things happen only when people envision a better tomorrow, decide what they truly want to make happen, and then act to turn their dreams into reality. This inner motivation to accomplish goals is important to organizational success.

There are three core processes of successful organizations. One of these, the entrepreneurial process, is based on the idea that individuals can and should take initiative. The successful organization is one which creates the environment and processes necessary to encourage employees to do so. In today's changing environment, what works today may not work tomorrow; therefore, employees who possess self-initiative and can work well without the cue system of job descriptions, can improve organizational responsiveness and success.

In a 1996 study by Bain and Company, 160 senior executives were surveyed to discover the attitudes, activities, and behaviors used to manage organizations.[1] Twenty-two percent of the CEO's responded that the management of human resources was the most important task of management. Developing and monitoring controls was the only task considered more important. According to authors Charles Farkas and Suzy Wetlaufer, the CEO's interviewed believe in order to "deflect and defeat the competition", management's imperative is to "hire and cultivate the kind of individuals who will act intelligently, swiftly, and appropriately without direct or constant supervision."[2]

Self-initiative by employees is important to organizational success. This characteristic results in faster response to issues and a more competitive organization. Self-initiative reduces the need for management follow-up, and is especially effective when employees are supportive of organizational goals and values.

A third characteristic of people that leads to organizational success is adaptability and flexibility. Success in the future depends on the ability of organizations to adopt and adapt to new technology. A flexible and adaptable work force can more successfully meet the challenges of changing technology and the changing business environment.

---

[1]Charles Farkas and Suzy Wetlaufer, May-June 1996, "The Ways Chief Executive Officers Lead," *Harvard Business Review* Vol. 74 (3), p. 110.
[2]Ibid, pp. 115-116.

Employee flexibility is a significant factor to success in a changing business environment. One of the top explanations for failure of individuals at the general manager level or higher is the inability to adapt during a transition. When the operations of a business are changing, or when companies evolve through merger and acquisition, those employees most resistant to change are often the first to be let go. Conversely, just as the inability to adapt to change can lead to failure, the ability of employees to adapt to new conditions and business methods can lead to organizational success.

While people are adapting to changes, taking initiative, and making competent decisions for business, employees can also improve the chances for success, by cooperating and coordinating efforts with other individuals and groups within the organization. The ability to coordinate diverse resources and develop cooperation within organizations is another characteristic of people, which leads to success.

The competency building process, mentioned earlier as one of the key processes of successful companies, both assumes and shapes an environment for collaborative behavior. Additionally, the ability to build teams and coordinate individual efforts is a source of competitive advantage.

Competency, self-motivation, and the ability to cooperate and adapt are all characteristics of people that will lead to successful organizations. These however, are not the only traits. The ability to be an entrepreneur, the ability to undertake and start something new, is not a necessity to organizational success; however, the possibilities of innovation and change are never realized until an idea is proposed by an individual.

Individuals also can have the characteristic of being quality focused. While a machine may be able to produce thousands of widgets each day without failure, it took an individual to develop the machine and do so with the expectation that it would produce quality results.

Another characteristic, somewhat related to an individual's expectation of quality, is that people possess vision. Almost everyone to varying degrees has some expectation of outcomes in life, or what quality represents. These expectations are an individual's vision. Before an organization can be truly successful, people within the organization must possess a vision of what expected outcome is desired.

When individuals possess vision, the next step in the process is to set goals, which are aligned with the vision. The next characteristic that can lead to organizational success, is that properly selected people will be supportive of organizational goals

In the business environment today, it is important for management to hire individuals who possess the previously mentioned characteristics. The technical aspects of the modern world require competent employees. The rapid technological change that occurs requires adaptability and flexibility by employees and management. Employees with quality-focus and self-initiative are better equipped to rapidly meet the needs of demanding customers. Employees who possess entrepreneurial characteristics are important to the ability to develop new products and services, and cooperative employees have the ability to coordinate efforts of diverse individuals and resources within the corporation in order to address competitive issues.

The strength of hiring and developing employees with these characteristics is that when the right person, with the desired characteristics, is accurately matched to a job or work group; competitiveness, and chances of success are improved. Knowledge workers can indeed improve organizational success. Once again, organizations can attempt to acquire knowledge workers from a competitor, do nothing and hope for the best (will they just appear), or organizations can actively develop knowledge workers.

FOUR

Creating Knowledge Workers to Improve Organizational Success

Presented with the preceding viewpoint, the attainment of knowledge workers should be the obvious goal of any organization. Knowledge workers, by definition, possess knowledge. Knowledge can be characterized in many different ways. Knowledge can be tacit (implied or unclear) or explicit. An individual can possess general knowledge or situational knowledge, specific to a certain context. Knowledge can be collective or individual. Knowledge can be about a subject;

person, place, or thing. There is knowledge of procedure or know-how. There is knowledge of the causal; know-why. Knowledge can be conditional; knowing what applies under certain conditions. There is also knowledge of the relational; knowledge of one type can provide insight or knowledge of another. Knowledge can be observable or non-observable. Knowledge can be positive, the knowledge of what works; as well as, negative, the knowledge of what does not work. Additionally, knowledge can be stand alone, functioning independently, or systematic, functioning as a part of a larger system.

Knowledge can be thought of as a combination of information and experience. Knowledge is embedded in context; it is acquired through one's own experience or reflections on the experience of others. If knowledge is separated from the context or experience, it turns into information, which can then be communicated independently from the experience. Information resides in media and networks; it is tangible. Knowledge resides in the experience, context, or relationship; it is intangible.

Knowledge is an elusive commodity, which is difficult to measure. In some ways knowledge is similar to industrial goods or natural resources. Knowledge can be divided among users: some students learn business while others learn physics.

Knowledge can be appropriated: military intelligence and business knowledge are often shared or appropriated on a need to know basis. Knowledge is scarce and not always universally available. Additionally, knowledge can depreciate in value or provide decreasing returns as it ages and becomes widespread.

In contrast, once knowledge is possessed, it is not likely to be taken away or re-allocated; the knower now knows. Once shared, the knowledge is acquired and subsequent allocations simply increase the knowers. Because knowledge can be disseminated it is not inherently scarce. In many cases the more knowledge is used, the more value it has, and rather than being non-renewable, knowledge once possessed often creates the condition and demand for the generation of new knowledge.

While knowledge itself is difficult enough to define, the act of creating knowledge workers seems almost impossible. However, if employees exist whom seem to fit the description of a knowledge worker, it would be possible to hypothesize what elements preceded the individual development. Through a review on the subject of knowledge workers and reflection on the personal experiences of individuals who I believe fit the description of a knowledge worker, I have made the following conclusion: there are thirteen key elements which lead to the creation or development of knowledge workers; most importantly, there exists one overall concept, which ties all of the elements together to allow organizations to develop knowledge workers to improve competitive success.

This theory is as follows. The resource an organization starts with is important to what can be achieved; therefore the first element is to have an appropriate hiring or selection process. Where new employees are placed is also important, the organizational environment must be managed effectively. Once employees are acquired, leadership, training, mentoring, and the implementation of processes leads to employee development. Additionally, an appropriate review and measurement process provides focus and further development. Over time, the eighth element, a knowledge worker is developed.

These eight elements, which lead to the development of the knowledge worker, should continue to be present to further facilitate development. However, to fully realize the value of knowledge workers, additional elements are required. Projects, such as the codification of knowledge, take advantage of individual knowledge and allow it to be transferred and further utilized. Employee attitudes must be understood and managed to facilitate achievement of organizational goals. Relationships of all kinds must be developed, and the gap between knowledge and action must be reduced. Lastly, the knowledge workers developed and whom benefits are derived from should be retained in order to provide continued future benefits.

The thirteen elements (the hiring process, the environment, leadership, training, mentoring, process development, review and measurement, time, project development, attitudes, relationships, action orientation, and retention) each require management focus and attention. The coordinated management of these elements is the overall concept, which leads to the development of knowledge workers and competitive success.

FIVE

<u>The Hiring Process</u>

A key component in the creation of any final product is the raw material. Creating knowledge workers is not an exception. The quality and character of new hires is important to the quality and the level of employee development ultimately achieved. This implies the hiring process is important and requires attention.

Through the hiring process, organizations acquire the raw material that is the employee. As mentioned previously, employees possess characteristics, which lead to organizational success. These characteristics are what make the raw material the employee represents, important. Some of the characteristics of people which lead to success and should be used for selection and promotion include; entrepreneurship, continually learning, self-initiative, cooperative, quality focused, adaptable, flexible, supportive of organizational goals, possessing vision, and participatory. Perhaps more importantly, new hires should possess explicit skills such as the ability to read, write, reason, or perform physical tasks as required by the position. In some instances where the desired skill is difficult to learn or duplicate, hiring someone with the pre-requisite skills is the only way to attain the knowledge.

Knowledge resides in the experience and expertise of individuals. Because knowledge requires individuals, it is logical that the individuals shape the knowledge and give it value. Individuals can make a difference and therefore the hiring of individuals is important. The initial knowledge an individual possesses, the reasoning skills acquired, and the ability to respond to new stimuli is an important aspect of the individual.

The process of selecting and hiring new employees can be very challenging. Successful hiring is not a science, and results can be achieved with various methods. However, there are actions, which can increase or decrease the likelihood of a successful hire. The process can be negatively impacted by common mistakes. By avoiding common mistakes and developing a systematic approach management can greatly increase the chances of hiring the right person.

One of the mistakes made in the hiring process is to be reactive to current or past events. Companies, should avoid being reactive. Hiring should not be based on a response to an open headcount, or an attempt to replicate or avoid the performance of a predecessor. Avoid unrealistic specifications. Superman is not filling the position, the result of unrealistic specifications is a reduced candidate pool and the possibility of ruling out legitimate candidates who may have the essential skills, but lack a specific consideration. Evaluate people in absolute terms. Review of prior performance for instance should be considered relative to context of the circumstances in which it was rendered. Do not accept candidates at face value. The prospective employee's objective is to be hired. People will readily provide examples of their best performance, while weaknesses and sometimes the truth are edited if not completely misrepresented. Companies should make a reasonable effort to validate prospective employee's statements and experience in the context of the desired resource to be acquired. The focus should be the future and the vision of the desired outcomes.

A second common mistake is to blindly believe references. While it is important to validate prospective employee's statements, it is also important to validate statements of others regarding the candidate or their relationship to the candidate. If you are a successful manager, avoid attempting to hire a replicate of yourself. Stereotyping, race, gender, nationality, or experience can lead to judgment errors. Delegating too much responsibility to human resources or other unprepared staff members provides the opportunity for failure. Time must be made for personal attention to the hiring process, whether participating in the actual process or briefing those responsible on the key issues and objectives desired.

Mistakes in hiring also exist in the failure to conduct structured interviews. Research indicates structured interviews are the most reliable of all popular techniques for predicting performance. A benefit of a structured interview process is the ability to help prevent the failure to acknowledge the emotional intelligence of the candidate. The lack of emotional IQ; self-awareness, self-regulation, motivation, empathy, and social skills, is largely related to failure, even when the individual possesses strength in IQ and experience. A structured interview process can also help eliminate politics and bias from decision making and helps to maintain focus on a predetermined objective.

Understanding the common hiring mistakes and taking action to improve the hiring process can make a real difference in the quality of the human resource. Making a good selection is not merely finding someone with the skills to do the job, but it includes such things as identifying the individual with the appropriate attitude or disposition. Similar to having a high emotional IQ, individuals should possess self-knowledge and the ability to see reality clearly and objectively.

The ability to bring the appropriate skills and attitude to an organization will increase the ability to continually clarify and deepen the focus and vision of the organization. This can provide for continuous evaluation and improvement which effectively is the basis of the learning organization. Therefore, the capabilities of the learning individuals are the basis for the capacity of the learning organization itself. Likewise the development of organizational knowledge is directly related to the development of the individual employees.

If individuals with emotional IQ and self- knowledge are desired, it is possible to identify these individuals based on characteristics which can be ascribed to a model. Individuals who seem to possess a sense of purpose, attention to detail, and the ability to prioritize effectively would seem to match the prototype. The ability to accept reality as an opportunity and the ability to embrace rather than resist change would demonstrate flexibility and openness. Knowing yourself (personal assets and limitations), and having an accurate view of others and the environment, as well as, how all three relate; is the most effective demonstration of emotional IQ.

Characteristics such as commitment, focus, patience, and capacity to learn can be identified. Looking at a prospective employee's history, experience, and behavior can provide insight. The more often and recent the behavior, the more likely the candidate is to possess the characteristic. Other characteristics which can be strong indicators of potential for success include: personal care, personal ownership, and trust. Each can be demonstrated or observed. Candidates who possess these characteristics have greater potential for success than those who do not.

The last characteristic is the ability and even disposition to build relationships and work with others. In a learning organization, a significant amount of the learning takes place as the result of interaction and observation of others. Additionally, once someone possesses knowledge, it is through relationships and interaction with others whereby the knowledge is passed on. Hiring individuals who can build relationships can develop an organization, which builds relationships. The learning organization develops the knowledge worker.

In order to facilitate the acquisition of the most valuable candidates, I suggest using a systematic approach to the hiring process. The first step is to define specifically what job or role needs to be performed. Next, identify the competencies and personality traits required for the specified needs. These characteristics can be associated to behaviors, education, and experiences. Actively searching for candidates who possess these characteristics and resisting reactive hiring in order to find the most qualified individual can virtually guarantee success. In Texas Hold'em, the term "outs" is used to describe the number of possible winning hands that could be drawn before all the cards are known. When individuals are hired, we are not capable of knowing all the possible outcomes. However, similar to poker, the greater the number of outs exist, the greater the probability of winning.

While job definition and accurately matching individuals to positions or roles is important to a systematic approach, the reverse analysis must also be performed. The question needs to be asked; does the role match the individual? Work must have meaning or life interest. For individuals, employment is an economic, a social, and a psychological relationship; a three legged stool which can only stand if all three adequately exist.

Ultimately, spending time and following a systematic approach leads to success. Performing the work to identify the needs to be met, defining the indicators of a desired candidate, searching for candidates, and conducting multiple interviews pay off in the end. The result is better hires and fewer turnovers. All of these duties are the responsibility of management, which leads us to what will become a recurring theme throughout the rest of this work, management plays an important role.

Quite a bit has been mentioned about the characteristics of individuals, which lead to success, and good hiring processes can improve the chances of selecting quality candidates. For employees to succeed, they must have "the 3 C's", capacity, capability, and commitment. Capacity is the basic ability, understanding, or skills necessary to fulfill a need. For example, individuals with poor communication skills seldom possess the capacity to become successful public relations managers. Capability is the ability of an individual to act on or apply themselves to something for which they have the capacity. Attaining the capability may require time and training or it may be as simple as being granted the authority. The last "C", commitment, is the psychological and emotional characteristic of the individual, which determines whether or how capabilities are applied.

There can be no capability without capacity, and all the capability in the world is worthless without commitment. In the hiring process, management can select committed individuals who already possess the needed capabilities or at minimum possess the capacity. In the words of Mike Ditka, Head Coach of the 1985 Superbowl Champion Chicago Bears, "You get good athletes who want to win, give them a system that maximizes their strengths, and work at it."[3] The key is to get individuals who want to win.

Because the quality of the human resource hired directly correlates to the productivity and the ability of the worker to utilize knowledge, management must focus time and energy on the hiring process. If knowledge workers are desired, hiring must be conducted in such a way as to maximize the likelihood of acquiring individuals who have the capacity to become knowledge workers in the given field.

Great organizations have something in common. They change the old adage "people are your most important asset" to "the *right* people are your most important asset". The real challenge for management is to hire employees who share the core organizational values; and create an environment that so strongly reinforces those values, that people who are not suitable either never get hired or move on in short order.

Getting the right people is what the hiring process is all about. The process of creating knowledge workers to improve organizational success starts with acquiring individuals with the capacity to become knowledge workers. Since management is the key link between the organization and the selection of the most

---

[3] Mike Ditka, 1995, "Many People One Goal," *Game Plans for Success* (NFL Properties Inc.) .

qualified individual, it is imperative that management makes the hiring process an area of focus, specifically with the creation of knowledge workers in mind.

SIX

Organizational Environment

Once management acquires the right individuals, it is important to place this raw resource in an appropriate environment. Just as high quality produce will lose value in a processing plant with no refrigeration, high quality employees will not reach their full potential for value in a poor organizational environment.

The importance of the environment or culture of an organization is a recurring theme in many management treatises. The organizational environment provides the physical and social structure to allow knowledge to be shaped into competency. Competency is a basic component of competitive advantage.

There are many aspects to environmental variables. Compensation, trust, camaraderie, training opportunities, freedom, security, benefits, responsibility, and many other factors impact the culture of an organization. Aspects of the culture or environment can either foster or repress the growth and exchange of knowledge, which is required to facilitate the creation of knowledge workers. There are five main environmental factors, which impact the development of a knowledge worker: freedom, purpose or direction, time constraints, sharing characteristics, and a support structure.

Freedom, represented by autonomy, encourages individual initiative and leads to improved success. While not every autonomous act is successful, many actions have desirable results and learning occurs with both success and failure. As such, freedom promotes experimentation and a diversity of ideas. Experiments are a crucial source of data and information. Knowledge and the creation of new knowledge is a direct result of the willingness to explore.

Management can unleash employee commitment by giving them the freedom to act, to try out their own ideas and be responsible for producing results. In the traditional hierarchical organization, the top thinks and the bottom acts. In a learning organization, thinking and acting must occur in every individual. An appropriate level of freedom and autonomy is a must. Ultimately, freedom is an environmental characteristic, which has significant impact on the existence of a learning organization and the creation of knowledge workers.

To be effective in creating knowledge, freedom must encourage some level of risk. With risk comes failure, and the culture must also be tolerant or forgiving of failure. If fear of failure inhibits the taking of risks, which accompany experimentation, innovation is discouraged. Not only is the knowledge gained from success lost, but also lost is the knowledge gained from failures. Failures resulting from risk can not be completely eliminated; however, if employees recognize the inherent possibility of failure can be forgiven, they are more apt to pursue innovation, which leads to knowledge development. It is important to note: a culture of forgiveness does not imply ignorance, only forgiveness of legitimate, non-repetitive mistakes. Management must embrace the concept of failing forward, and eliminating fear in the organizational environment.

While freedom or autonomy is important; empowerment without vision, or freedom without responsibility, is incoherent. The second desirable environmental characteristic, a sense of purpose or direction, is important to ensure increased freedom does not become counter-productive. Clarity of focus, by management as well as individual employees, rather than rules and structure, provides greater control of the organization. Clarity of focus is provided through goals, leadership, and vision, all of which should be present in the organizational environment to encourage the development of knowledge workers.

The third environmental influence is to establish an appropriate level of urgency, and time constraints. It is imperative to have project goals, project timeframes, and some level of performance pressure. In order to establish an appropriate sense of urgency and clarify the importance of time as a resource; management should provide an environment where the focus is not only get it done, but "get it done well and learn from what you do".

Employees do not exist in a vacuum; they come and go in organizations through the normal processes of hiring, attrition, and retirement. While they are employed they attend work, they participate in the organizational environment. People contribute and interact. If knowledge exists ultimately within individuals, as individuals participate in the organization, experimenting and making decisions, sharing experience and results with others, knowledge is created and shared. This shared context "knowledge' is dynamic and changes over time.

The action by employees to create shared context by explaining, challenging, and aligning points of view, does not occur instantaneously. This activity requires systematic attention, and a reasonable amount of time. Perhaps the most effective explanation of time as a resource and necessary environmental asset can be found in this daily interaction of employees. Creating knowledge requires management and employees to engage in open, honest, constructive, and reflective dialogue. Knowledge is a direct outcome of experience, reflection, and dialogue, and these activities require that most precious managerial asset: time. Few organizations budget directly for these activities, yet little knowledge is ever developed without them. Developing an organizational environment where individuals are encouraged to take time to experience, reflect, and communicate, establishes the basis for a learning organization.

In addition to the recognition of time as a resource and the importance of this resource to the environment, the fourth element, sharing characteristics, is at the root of the concept of developing shared context.

The importance of sharing, and developing a culture in which interaction and exchange is the norm, is demonstrated by the following. Consider the situation in which a group of people with diversity of ideas and experience almost always outperforms an individual. The individual is limited to viewing his or her environment from his or her perspective and experience. The group on the other hand, can share perspectives, experience, and ideas. This inherently leads to fresh viewpoints and new ways of thinking. As a result of sharing, the group can experience synergies not available to the individual.

This idea of sharing reminds me of an old saying that goes something like this: if you and I each have a penny and we exchange them, we each still have a penny, but if you and I each have an idea and we share them, we now each have twice as many ideas. In the context of the learning organization, anytime an individual has the opportunity to see things from a new perspective, or experience something new through the experience of others, the learning process has occurred. A culture of sharing allows everyone to learn and grow, and the outcome of such a process has to be a much richer and more diverse sense of what is going on and what needs to be done.

The final environmental element is the existence of a support structure. While there have always been individuals who excel, all individuals within an organization cannot be expected to achieve peak performance with regards to developing and utilizing organizational knowledge without external influence. There are many steps that can be taken in this regard, but the most important step is to acknowledging that one cannot build a learning organization on a foundation of inexperience, strained personal relationships, distractions, and insecurity. Organizations need to support workers in maintaining their personal lives, in order to prevent personal lives from impacting work, and thereby maximizing the employee's ability to focus on work issues.

The successful learning organization actively supports employees not only to balance work and home, but also to develop the individual as a valuable, contributing member of the work family as well. Individuals with the support of the organization can achieve self-actualization, they can improve their living conditions, and they can increase personal satisfaction. With the support of the organization, employees can develop a sense of empowerment, the sense of accomplishment, and many other personal interests. Developing a culture or environment where individuals feel supported and nurtured allows the organization to maintain morale and reduce turnover, both of which increase the longevity of the employee and the ability to develop into a knowledge worker.

Learning communities thrive in a culture that supports sharing knowledge; the key is for management to create an environment where knowledge sharing is truly valued. Sharing must be acknowledged and rewarded, and barriers: untrustworthy behavior, constant competition, imbalances in giving and receiving, and the "that's not my job" attitude must be deterred.

Research suggests the tendency for knowledge to spread easily reflects not only suitable technology, but suitable social contexts, both are manageable. What an individual knows is what they believe, in order to pass their knowledge to others, they must share their beliefs. In order to do this, individuals must present ideas to others and justify them. This requires the feeling of acceptance, a characteristic directly related to openness and a management established environment.

Management has a direct influence on many aspects of the environment. The censorship of individuals does not add to innovation. Individuals rewarded for hoarding knowledge will do so. If expertise is rewarded, but mentoring is not, people will not surrender power, especially when sharing tacit knowledge takes time and personal contact. Inequality of status can reduce interaction, as well as, distance. Emotional disagreement in contrast to intellectual disagreement can result in reduced interaction between individuals. In order to manage these issues in the environment, ideas must be heard, valued, and targeted.

Management of the organizational environment is more than picking people and providing structure, the entire process must be managed. The strategy structure system theory of management with a hierarchical, highly structured environment made possible the growth of huge corporations, but that it is no longer as effective in today's competitive environment. Vertical processes have started to be replaced by horizontal processes in order to achieve better results. Today's organizations are often less about structure than they are about three main processes: the entrepreneurial process, the competency building process, and the renewal process.

The entrepreneurial process is the externally oriented, opportunity-seeking attitude that motivates employees to run their operations as if they owned them. In this process, upper management must realize that it is not always in the best position to exercise the entrepreneurial initiative. The organization should not be built for top-down direction and delegation, but rather to give support to bottom-up ideas and initiative.

In order to provide the foundation for such a structure, management must show that they trust and value the employees as well as their ideas. Employees must feel that what they have to offer has value or they will not bother to take the initiative. At the same time, management must also impart some sort of self-discipline to the employees, in order to provide direction and commitment to the organizational goals.

The second process is the competence-building process. In the global market place, it is no longer acceptable to merely match the flexibility and responsiveness of competitors. Organizations must also exploit and leverage the diverse resources that exist in individual frontline units, in order to take advantage of the talents and knowledge that resides in individual employees. Management should create an environment in which employees are challenged to create, develop and diffuse competencies throughout the organization.

The third process, the renewal process, is designed to challenge companies' strategies and the assumptions behind them. It uses knowledge existing at the frontline of the organization to formulate policies rather than having top management form policies based on information that has been filtered through several layers of hierarchy. It is a continuous process at all levels of reviewing the status quo and asking, how our business can be improved today.

In conclusion, the strategy, structure, systems model of organizational design would be better off being replaced with a purpose, process, people model, in order to shape the behaviors of people and create an environment that enables them to take initiative, to cooperate, and to learn.

Organizational culture may be the biggest impediment to knowledge transfer, this obstacle however; can indeed be overcome, by more deliberate management. While there can be no single best method, structure, or organizational design to develop knowledge workers, management can guide the organizational environment to create a learning organization. By providing focus and direction, encouraging freedom and responsibility, providing the resource of time, through encouraging the sharing of information and ideas, and by supporting and nurturing individuals; learning is increased.

SEVEN

Leadership, Vision, and Goals

Perhaps the most important element in the development of knowledge workers is leadership. Leadership comes in two forms: power or self-interest driven and responsibility or group-interest driven. Power driven leadership is interested in short-term gain, knowledge as power, controlled information flow, and self focus. Responsibility driven leadership, on the other hand, is interested in long-term sustained growth, building a learning environment, sharing and skill building, and a focus on others.

What could be a better element for the development of knowledge workers, than responsibility driven leadership? Where can organizations find effective leaders? True leadership emerges, and natural leaders are often the most effective. In everyday life, where people are deciding, acting, and doing, we know who the leader is and why they are there. The leaders; whether formal or informal, appointed or not, emerge from the group. Not by self-assertion, but because they make sense in the context of what is needed. The challenge for management and the organization is to identify and cultivate natural, responsibility driven leaders, and get them into the positions which optimize their capabilities.

There are several characteristics of effective leadership which can be identified. Leadership is values based, a leader's values provide the basis for his vision, and a leader's vision is represented by goals. Effective leadership is able to gain commitment and compliance, and effective leadership is committed to developing others.

Values provide the basis for vision, and ultimately goals, as they are the simple guiding principles people live by. Values in a sense define who people are as individuals. Who individuals are and how they view the world, significantly impacts actions, how people lead, and what they aspire to accomplish. These values and goals; combined with the competency to act, guide the operation and are a real source of independence from the environment. When the environment demands a new response, they provide a reference point for change. Ultimately, changes (to include learning) are driven by our values.

Effective leadership possesses values, knows what values they possess, and communicates the values to others. Effective leadership also ensures values are consistent within an organization; otherwise, the organization will lack coherence.

Vision is the extension of values. Individuals form mental models of how things are and how things should be, based on individual values. And while no one can give another his vision and values, others can be encouraged to develop shared values, and vision can be successfully shared. The individual's vision can be shared with others to form a shared vision. Shared vision, the result of leadership; provides direction, guidance, and goals for an organization. Furthermore; because know-how without purpose or application is a wasted asset, the vision also provides the philosophy of why before how. Leadership, possessing vision, establishes objectives and facilitates action; this leads directly to both learning and improved performance.

Goals and objectives are the physical representation of leadership's vision. Much has been written on the subject of objective setting for improved performance: management texts, how-to books, and other media will ensure this topic will continue to get attention in the future.

Whether creating a corporate strategy or planning what to have for dinner, the act of planning serves to organize thoughts or vision and define action to achieve an expected outcome. Anyone who has been involved in a group, which had no clear objective, probably found that the group was spending a good deal of time responding to the external environment. Since there was no clear outcome expected, there was probably not a clear plan of action, and the result was rather than having internal forces proactively drive the organization the organization was responding and reacting moment to moment to external factors. This type of activity can lead to a dysfunctional organization, counter-productive actions, poor performance, and low productivity. By setting objectives, organizations improve the chances of success and provide a means of grading performance.

Effective objectives exhibit a number of characteristics. Goals should be specific, concise, realistic, flexible, and easy to understand. They should be measurable and have some time component, and goals should reflect a desire for above-standard performance. Effectively implemented, goals provide direction, guidance for day to day activities, a reference for change, and focus individuals on productive tasks. Goals reduce ambiguity, make decision making easier, and through achievement, enhance motivation.

Improved performance results from the individual's better understanding of their position and how it inter-relates to other parts of the organization. In the process of defining and setting objectives, an individual learns more about not only the task assigned, but also why it is important and how it affects other parts of the organization. Setting objectives also facilitates learning, when evaluation is being conducted to monitor performance. This is an opportunity for individuals to learn what is and is not working. Understanding where one is going and how they are going to get there makes the process of getting there more effective and efficient.

Applying the concept of goal setting to leadership and the development of knowledge workers, it would seem logical that leaders can value knowledge, envision how to increase and utilize knowledge, and develop objectives or goals to guide the organization in pursuit of the development of knowledge workers.

Organizations can focus on the management of information and knowledge to enhance organizational performance. Knowledge is the fundamental basis of competition. Competing successfully on knowledge requires either aligning goals to what the organization and individual's know already, or developing the knowledge and the capabilities within the individual's, needed to support a desired objective. In this process, leadership, vision, and goals have a direct impact on the development of knowledge workers.

Goals alone will not achieve the desired results. Leadership is necessary to attain commitment to the goals. I am sure everyone reading this book can attest to personal experience with workers who lack commitment or were not always working as hard as they could. Employees who do not work to their potential, do not demonstrate commitment. Without commitment throughout the organization, the organization's full potential cannot be realized, and leadership is the key link to gaining commitment.

Leadership plays the greatest role in gaining commitment as individuals must be enrolled in a vision and not sold on the idea. Individuals learn most effectively when they have a genuine sense of responsibility for their actions. People learn what they need to learn, not what someone else thinks they need to learn. This reinforces the idea leadership is needed to communicate the importance of learning to the individual, in order that the individual will understand how important learning is to their own benefit and commit to, or enroll, in the vision and goals of the organization.

Commitment over an extended period of time is important to learning. Leadership is important to ensure commitment over time, and provide some mechanism for control in the event individuals deviate from the desired objectives. Management should succeed in maintaining focus, rather than hands-on control. Through focus on objectives, leaders create the flexibility and responsiveness that every organization needs. Leaders shape their organizations through concepts, not through elaborate rules or structures.

Improving individual commitment will reduce the need for control by the organization. This does not however imply all control should be through ideas only. Leadership should also monitor performance relative to goals and objectives. Having goals provides a reference point for change. In the event individuals stray from the desired objective, leadership should be aware of the situation and action should be taken to correct or address the issue. This act of ensuring compliance itself is a learning process.

Leadership, vision and goals lead to employee development and learning. Refer again to the idea of responsibility driven leadership being interested in long-term sustained growth, building a learning environment, encouraging sharing and skill building, and a focus on others. This concept embodies the idea that effective leadership develops knowledge workers. In a learning organization, leaders are designers and teachers. They are responsible for building organizations, continually expanding their capabilities, clarifying the vision, and improving the shared mental models. In short, they are responsible for learning.

For an individual to be successful and develop into a knowledge worker, they need "The Three C's": capacity, capability, and commitment. Effective leadership seeks individuals with the capacity ..., develops the capability..., and maintains the commitment to facilitate continuous learning and the application of knowledge for success.

Leadership sets the tone for a culture of learning and sharing. Leadership encourages organizational trust, caring, and the pursuit of new knowledge. Leadership works to develop dialogue and beneficial relationships between individuals and groups. Leadership pursues continuous self-refinement and process improvement through performance reviews, training, job sharing, and OJT. Leadership facilitates the acquisition and development of technology as well as processes to provide for the codification and sharing of existing knowledge. Leadership can lead by example and encourage and promote the leadership skills of others; and leadership can reward, punish, and give promotions based on adherence to the values and goals of the organization.

These are just a few of the actions leadership takes which directly impact the development of individuals, but they are by no means the limit. An effective leader understands that his job is not to know everything and decide everything, but rather to create an environment in which there are lots of people who both know and do. Leaders achieve this through actions in word and deed.

Ultimately, leadership, vision, and goals have a significant impact on the development of knowledge workers. Therefore, managing these items would logically increase the likelihood of success in having knowledge workers develop. Management must demonstrate they value individual leadership; natural leaders should be sought out, promoted, and supported. Management must continuously communicate the message that knowledge, learning, and development are valued and they are being evaluated.

Additionally, management can demonstrate leadership by communicating a vision of a learning organization and setting goals, which are compatible with developing knowledge workers. Lastly, the management of leadership, vision, and goals can be summed up as follows: If you can visualize it, you can measure it; and if you can measure it, you can manage it.

EIGHT

Training/Learning

The fourth element, which leads to the development of knowledge workers, is training. The importance of training is evident, not only for the obvious benefits of improving the capabilities of individuals and teams, but also because training is an element which is highly correlated to employee satisfaction and retention. Training helps employee's to feel competent and improves confidence in their capabilities. A satisfied employee, with greater longevity in their position or role, in an environment, which provides continuos training, is hard-pressed not to increase their knowledge.

The reason training is effective in developing knowledge workers is training allows individuals to learn from the experience and knowledge of others. With training, individuals no longer have to repeat the same failures as others, and success does not need to be rediscovered.

Training provides a context for data and information. Successful knowledge creation is about changing data and information into decision and action. The process whereby training develops into knowledge is learning, and it is precisely learning which allows for the development of the knowledge worker. Organizations learn only through individuals who learn, yet individual learning does not guarantee organizational learning. Organizational learning requires individual learning to be shared, without it no organizational learning occurs, and training directly impacts individual learning.

Learning allows companies to get better over time or continually improve, and continuous improvement has been credited with decreased cycle time, decreased cost, reduced inventory, improved quality, speeding distribution, and improving customer satisfaction to name a few. Ultimately, the ability to learn is a competitive advantage, and training increases learning.

Training, especially OJT, develops context specific knowledge for the firm. Learning from experience and the knowledge embedded in organizational routines tends to be unique, specific, and difficult to duplicate. This leads to sustainability of the competitive advantage. Learning also leads to what this author refers to as "The Leap of Knowledge". Individuals, who gained expertise on a subject, can often link disparate pieces of information, which may seem unrelated to less experienced individuals. They "Leap" to solutions and opportunities, which only they could, as a result of their knowledge.

Learning occurs in many ways and has many sources: dialogue, on line networks, group-ware, documentation, databases, mentors, colleagues, experience, OJT, active participation, and experimentation to name a few. Knowledge resides in individuals, behaviors, procedures, software, equipment, publications, universities, government agencies, professional associations, consultants, venders, and practices and processes, virtually everywhere. Most workplace learning is not actually even planned. In most cases, learning goes on unbudgeted, unplanned, and un-captured by the organization, it is acquired in an informal manner, resides in the individual and is often not shared. In order to develop knowledge workers; training and learning, whether formal or informal should be encouraged, documented, and shared.

Training should be managed, to optimize the effectiveness of the learning process. The type of knowledge or information being trained or communicated determines which training methods are most appropriate. A simple example of this is the characteristic of knowledge being either tacit or explicit. Tacit knowledge is less teachable and observable. Tacit knowledge is often complex and relational. It is less visible, less expressible, and more personal such as insight and intuition.

Explicit knowledge is more easily teachable, observable, simple, and independent. Explicit knowledge is easier to capture, codify, distribute, and measure. Often, explicit knowledge is in the form of words, numbers, data, formula, manuals, etc.... Training explicit knowledge is often easier and cheaper, while tacit knowledge is more difficult and costly to train.

Explicit knowledge lends itself to the process of codification and distribution, often training on explicit knowledge can take the form of providing individuals with manuals or documentation. Tacit knowledge, on the other hand, is more likely to require relationship building. An individual, who needs to learn, must spend time or develop a relationship with an individual who is knowledgeable. In this manner, learning is either process based or relationship based. By managing the training methods, organizations can improve the transfer of knowledge from those who have to those who have not.

Perhaps the best example of the training of tacit knowledge is the apprenticeship.

The training/learning in an apprenticeship is dependent on the relationship that is established. The face to face interaction and the sharing of information and perspectives make up the training experience. The nature of the relationship can have significant impact on the quality of the finished craftsman. Building and maintaining effective relationships is important to the learning process.

Relationships are less important, though not completely irrelevant, in the training of explicit knowledge. When training explicit knowledge, it is more important to identify, locate, and transfer existing knowledge cheaply and rapidly, usually in some form of written communication. It is not coincidental that the Roman word for tribes without a written language was barbarian, and history is dominated by cultures, which lead in the development and utilization of the written word.

Perhaps the best example of training explicit, process based knowledge is the codification and sharing of "best practices". Taking developed knowledge, which exists in the best practice and sharing or training it throughout the organization facilitates learning and knowledge development. Think about the quality movement of the 1980's and '90's, organizations were attempting to identify and replicate their best practices, they often discovered best practices were unnoticed and under-utilized in other parts of the organization. This is often still the case today. Best practice replication can be achieved by locating, transferring, and using the existing knowledge. Training and learning are a direct result of the transfer of knowledge, and the transfer of best practices is one of the most tangible examples of knowledge management.

The sharing of best practice is not often easy. Even when recognized, best practices can often take a significant amount of time to be transferred or adopted throughout the organization. There are three main reasons for this phenomenon. One, there is a lack of knowledge by both knowers and those who need to know, that the knowledge either exists or is needed. Two, a lack of capacity, resources, or practical details prevents implementation. Lastly, personal relationships between the knowers and those who need to know do not exist or are not sufficiently strong enough to facilitate the transfer. This seems to validate the necessity to provide both the explicit, codified knowledge and the development of relationships, for effective training and learning to be achieved.

In the example of training through the apprenticeship, knowledge creation was a result of building a relationship to transfer information. It is difficult to believe that at no time is some explicit direction given. Similarly, in the best practice example, explicit knowledge is transferred, and it is highly likely that a tacit dimension exists in some of the knowledge, which requires relationship building.

Authors Nonaka and Konno state "knowledge creation is a spiraling process of interactions between explicit and tacit knowledge."[4] They have developed a model for knowledge creation, which they refer to as the SECI Model, which stands for socialization, externalization, combination, and internalization. This model is referenced on the following page.

---

[4] Ikujiro Nonaka, and Noboru Konno. Spring 1998. "The Concept of "Ba": Building a Foundation for Knowledge Creation." *California management Review* Vol. 40 (3), p. 42.

Figure 1: Spiral Evolution of Knowledge Creation

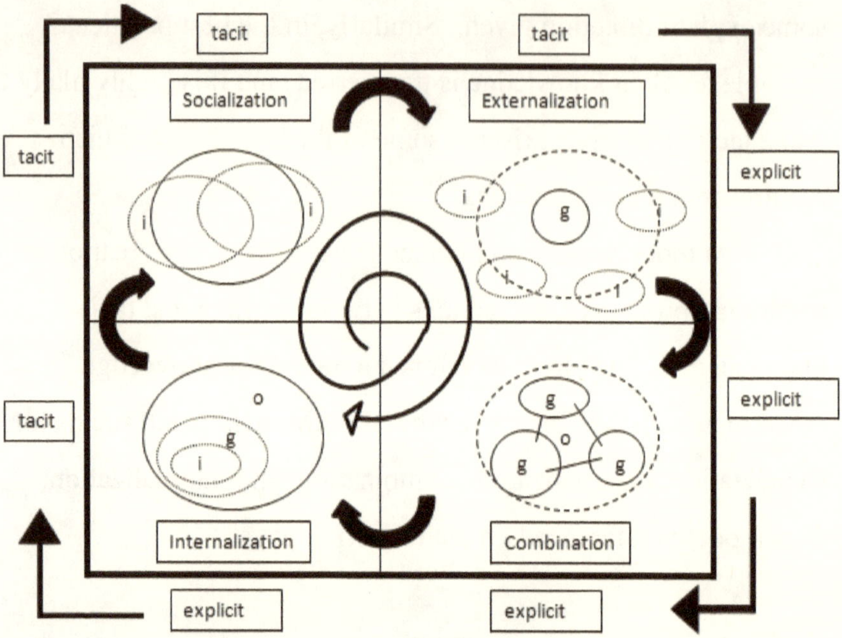

i: individual, g: group, o: organization

SOURCE: Nonaka and Konno, p. 43.

The knowledge creation process starts with socialization. Individuals share experience, information, and tacit, personal knowledge. In this phase, knowledge is both gained by the individual and disseminated to other individuals. The second stage is externalization. Individuals interact with the group. Personal, tacit knowledge is expressed and translated. Philosophies are shared, as well as facts. Individuals commit to the group, and in this phase, the individual knowledge becomes group knowledge.

The third stage is combination. This stage is a key to the process of communication and diffusion of the group knowledge. In this stage, existing and new knowledge is captured, edited, justified, integrated, and disseminated. This results in explicit, communicable, meaningful, and usable knowledge. The final stage is internalization. Explicit knowledge created in stage three is applied, and the learning through doing process allows the individual to develop new explicit and tacit knowledge. This leads back to stage one and provides a continuous cycle of training, learning, and knowledge creation.

Comparing the SECI Model to the concept of training in order to develop knowledge workers; both have the same objective, and each must address the issues associated with tacit and explicit knowledge. Ultimately, implementing the model could be considered a form of training. The model itself seems to be merely an observation of the typical learning process. The individual needs information they do not have, socializes his issue with a friend or knowledgeable source, gains understanding or new perspective, uses the new perspective to become informed, and then acts on the new information. This is seemingly a natural process.

So, what makes the difference? Creating knowledge is not as simple as starting a training program, implementing the SECI Model, or hoping your employees are just naturally inquisitive. Management must take an active role in facilitating the development of individuals through training. As mentioned earlier, people learn what they need to learn, management must provide guidance as to what is needed. People learn best when they have a genuine sense of responsibility for their actions, because of this human characteristic, management must develop an environment in which individuals feel accountable for the success of their training and learning process. Additionally, management must facilitate the resources and nurture the relationships, which are required to maximize the training environment.

Management can help to guide the training process in several ways. Actively scanning the environment for changes can identify future training needs. Instituting performance benchmarking to continually monitor historical performance can help identify areas where remedial or additional training may be required. By implementing continuous improvement teams, new methods and procedures can be developed and implemented into training. As mentioned earlier, the sharing of best practices can be stressed to improve the transfer rate within the organization.

Each of these activities is directly impacted by the involvement of management.

Management can establish the commitment to learning and the importance of training, through the role of reward and punishment. If a manager values the individual who continues to learn, and an environment of sharing information and developing knowledge is desired, then a system must be set up to encourage, enable, and reward those behaviors which achieve this goal and discourage that which is counter-productive. The Manager's task is to design a learning process, and training should be part of this process.

NINE

Mentorship

The fifth element, which leads to the development of knowledge workers, is mentorship. Similar to leadership and the apprenticeship role of training, mentorship provides guidance and instruction. Mentorship can set a standard and demonstrate through word and deed not only a way to work, but also a way to live.

A mentor can be compared to an advisor, a teacher, or a coach. Their role is not only to provide knowledge of an event or subject, but also to show how the subject relates to the whole. In the mentorship, knowledge is derived from the relationship between a knower and an individual. Mentoring allows the individual to take advantage of the life experience, and knowledge, of the more experienced knower. Mentorship is most important in areas where there is no clear correct answer, and mentorship is often more about providing perspective rather than solutions.

Socially, it seems to be a natural occurrence that people seek to get advice from friends, family, and others in the community. Often, people seek an elder or someone whom they know has experience in the area in which they are seeking advice. This in effect is a mentoring relationship, which occurs naturally. The same relationships exist naturally in workplace settings.

In order to help develop knowledge workers, organizations should try to promote and expand existing mentoring relationships. By formalizing mentoring and defining a clear responsibility for senior members of the organization to help junior members; junior members grow and develop. Additionally, the organization increases the transfer of knowledge. Since knowledge is to a large extent equated with power and influence, individuals will often attempt to increase their value by hording their knowledge. Under such circumstances, mentoring processes must improve individual access to expertise in the company. Management can achieve this by defining two responsibilities for the individual: the responsibility to acquire expertise; and the responsibility to make your expertise accessible to others. Employees must understand that they are responsible for sharing knowledge. Mentoring is all about more knowledgeable people helping less knowledgeable people become more knowledgeable. Management can encourage this practice by communicating the importance and the responsibility for the individual to participate to the processes to acquire and share knowledge.

Mentoring programs may not be successful with all employees based on their expertise level or attitude, yet for most, being mentored contributes to the knowledge development process, and mentoring itself can provide a growth experience and improved relations in the workplace. Both of which can add value to the employee experience, leading to greater satisfaction and increased longevity.

Returning to the idea that knowledge is developed through experience and training, mentoring facilitates knowledge creation. The lack of mentoring not only misses the opportunity to increase knowledge, but risks losing any knowledge already created if the employee leaves for greener pastures.

For management to facilitate knowledge development through mentoring programs, they must first recognize mentoring relationships have value, measure it, reward it, and act on it. If individuals are rewarded for hoarding knowledge, they will do so.

If expertise is rewarded but mentoring is not, people will not surrender power. Policies, which increase the number and quality of mentoring relationships, must be pursued, and sharing of knowledge and expertise must be rewarded.

While mentorship itself is hard to measure, the skills gained through mentoring can be assessed. Individuals can be judged by their performance, which is an indicator of the successfulness of the mentoring relationship. Management can then act on the performance information to work to improve the mentoring programs. Ultimately, management must come to realize mentors and mentorship needs to be nurtured, supported, enhanced, and cared for.

TEN

Processes

In the discussion of the organizational environment, the concept of the purpose, process, people model was identified as a method to shape the behaviors of people and create an environment that enables them to take initiative, to cooperate, and to learn. Significant here is the following idea: processes are developed and refined, by people, for the purpose of achieving goals and meeting objectives. We can further build on this by stating the repetition of processes and the modification of these processes for the purpose of process improvement, results in greater learning and the further development of knowledge.

Knowledge resides in the processes and routines of daily business. Processes provide a method for completion of task, and can be readily communicated to others. If adequately documented, even inexperienced individuals can implement processes. The action of working through the process becomes educational. Additionally, in the case of the experienced worker, the act of working through a process provides the opportunity to improve upon the process. Continuous process improvement ultimately results in greater competitiveness.

When properly implemented, processes have been proven to increase performance. Processes do this by providing guidance for day to day activities. Processes provide direction as to which actions are the most appropriate, and processes focus individuals on productive tasks. Processes provide for reduced ambiguity and increased alignment between actions and organizational goals. Processes can even impact motivation in the sense that individuals know what they will be judged against and the process provides a clear sense of required responsibilities.

Repetition of a process allows an individual to learn the process in detail and start to understand how the process relates to the system as a whole, to other processes, and to other individuals. In this respect, processes fulfill the role of training, learning, and the development of the knowledgeable worker.

The utilization of processes as a learning mechanism is consistent with the internalization process described in the SECI model. Explicit knowledge embodied in action and practice becomes personal knowledge, which in turn can be shared and improved upon. As is the case with training, the codification of knowledge in the format of processes and routines is important for acquired knowledge and best practice to be shared and contribute to further learning by others in the organization..

Management must recognize the development and utilization of processes promotes learning, leads to the development of knowledge workers, and increases competitiveness. Management must also recognize what is needed to provide for processes in the environment. While it is true that some employees will, if left alone, develop their own processes; it is important for management to encourage and guide the development of processes to ensure this tool is utilized and the results align with goals. It is also imperative to promote the improvement and dissemination of processes, which are effective.

In addition to promoting the development of processes for day to day activities, management can increase process knowledge in the firm, by developing processes, which get employees to take the time to codify and articulate existing processes and knowledge. This could be as simple as requiring, activity logs and documentation of simple process flows; or as complex as requiring white papers or documentation of significant projects. The act of producing the output provides a history and reinforces what was learned by the individual. In addition, codification puts the knowledge in a form that can be communicated, reviewed, and evaluated.

Management should develop processes to allow the organization to get the right knowledge in the right hands at the right time. Systems and processes can be developed to record, index, and make accessible the company and job specific knowledge, which is created daily. The process must be more than just dumping data in a repository; the process must be made meaningful and useful to those involved.

Developing a meaningful documentation process is perhaps the most significant and common problem in efforts to create a knowledge-sharing environment. This is made easier today with electronic media and searchable databases, but even the best tools cannot overcome a poor strategy or lack of focus. While the concept of a powerful database or an all-inclusive knowledge center is good, if there are problems with the usefulness, the value is diminished. Failure of the system being designed will result in wasted time and capital. Again, it is important for the data, information, and knowledge to be meaningful and useful to both those who would be using it, as well as, those who would be contributing.

In addition to developing process for day to day activities, and processes to document and share the existing knowledge; Management should also support and develop processes, which result in the development and maintenance of personal relationships. Documentation processes, linking people together with technology, and other methods to transfer knowledge often fail without the development of relationships between the individual who possesses knowledge and the individual or group seeking information. Often, someone who knows the answer is sitting right next to someone who needs the answer.

Developing relationships provides the link needed to share knowledge, which is neither obvious nor easy to document. Processes or routines, which lead to the development of relationships, include regularly scheduled staff meetings, the creation of multi-departmental teams to review issues and process impacts, and can even include informal company gatherings. Relationships do not have to be limited to internal employees, but could also extend to vendors, customers, and the general public. Processes such as formal, scheduled, job specific training and degree programs provide individuals with opportunity to interact with others outside of the organization.

In order to achieve the most benefit from process knowledge, management must manage, develop, and continuously improve the processes of the organization. Management must develop processes to facilitate the codification, indexing, and distribution of knowledge, and management must institute processes and routines, which facilitate the development of relationships, important to the sharing of knowledge, both within and outside the organization.

In order to accomplish this task and ensure processes are developed and followed, people need incentives to participate. Management needs to develop a system, which encourages individuals to follow existing processes, continuously improve these processes, and document and share process information. The ability to follow processes, improve processes, and the level and quality of employee contribution to process documentation are all subject to review and appraisal. The ability to demonstrate the establishment of personal relationships for the direct sharing of knowledge, while more difficult to measure, is also subject to review when it comes time for annual compensation. If management does not make expectations clear, and reward desired behaviors, individuals will not likely go out of their way to develop and improve processes on their own.

If individuals are not developing and improving processes currently, and if process knowledge is not being shared today; then codification and technology solutions will not likely help.

Individuals must understand the importance and significance of process knowledge; and management is integral to communicate, demonstrate, and facilitate this understanding, in order to achieve the desired outcome: the development of knowledge workers and improved competitiveness.

ELEVEN

Review and Measure

The next element, which leads to the development of knowledge workers, is the process of review and measurement. Recall, the importance of self-knowledge as mentioned in chapters six and seven. Self-knowledge, the personal recognition of one's own values, strengths, weaknesses and expertise, is important in new hires, as it is a sign of a high emotional IQ and personal mastery. Also, self-knowledge is important to goal setting, leadership, and vision, as it is the means by which individuals and organizations recognize where they are and what they must do to get where they want to be. While self-knowledge is important to both of these topics, it is the basis for the importance of review and measurement.

Self-reference, the recognition of one's current situation relative to the environment, guides change in action and behavior for both individuals and organizations, and review and measurement provides individuals and organizations with knowledge of self, which can be used to learn, grow, and increase competitiveness.

Review and measurement of knowledge and its development may seem difficult, yet much is measurable. Even in chaos theory, systems, which are random and unpredictable, seem to exist within measurable boundaries. When reviewing knowledge, the use of knowledge, and knowledge creation; both subjective and objective measures can be identified.

Managers can judge the amount and quality of knowledge being communicated, as well as, the output and production of those using knowledge. In addition, behaviors and skills can be observed regarding who is using and sharing knowledge. The amount of information being generated, the frequency of accessing knowledge sources, and the value of the information to various users are each measurable characteristics of knowledge.

Of all the possible measurable characteristics, related to knowledge and knowledge management, the two found to be most important are the measurement of performance and the measurement of attitudes and the environment.

The main benefits from measuring performance are the ability to ensure compliance to goals and objectives and the ability to benchmark performance. Compliance to goals and objectives is important to organizational success. The entire purpose of establishing organizations and developing businesses, with the exception of Government agencies and not for profit groups, is to achieve goals and objectives mostly centered on some aspect of profitability. A goal without compliance, much like freedom without responsibility, is irresponsible. Adhering to established best-practices and pursuing process improvement, in order to meet organizational goals, establishes a situation in which learning occurs. Measurement of performance is an indicator of how well processes are being followed and how much new learning has occurred.

Benchmarking performance, as mentioned previously, leads to learning and is the basis for the transfer of best practice. Measurement and review for the purpose of benchmarking directly impacts learning. In most cases, efforts to improve organizational performance depend largely on implementing what is already known or some variation of previously successful actions. The benchmarking aspect of the performance measurement and review process assists managers to identify what is known; this helps to provide focus on what is needed for success and areas in which further learning is desired, thereby influencing the learning process.

In addition to measuring performance, attitudes and the environment should be reviewed and measured. Employee's who are satisfied with their work and find their job fulfilling and rewarding are less likely to leave an organization and more likely to actively participate in their work. Active participation in a position or company, over an extended period of time provides an opportunity for learning and knowledge development. An awful lot can be said for just showing up and paying attention.

Monitoring the environment for signs such as low participation in meetings, low creativity, the existence of cliques, and reduced interaction by employees with management can indicate individual attitudes or the environment are not conducive to satisfied employees or a learning organization. Even little changes such as employees who do not smile much or who rush to leave the building everyday can be indicators of an environment or attitude which may need attention.

In reference to individual attitudes towards work and creating a learning organization, there are several levels of individual commitment, ranging from apathy, to compliance, to full commitment. Ultimately, to realize knowledge development, individuals and organizations must be committed to learning. Individual action and attitudes demonstrate the level of this commitment, and through the measurement and review process, attitudes and the environment can be better understood and managed to facilitate the development of a learning organization.

Review and measurement alone are not enough. The key is to act on the knowledge gained through the review and measurement process. Learning, sharing, contribution, and participation can all be evaluated. Individual performance and the value of projects and processes can be determined, but unless this knowledge is acted on, little benefit is gained.

In order for the measurement process to be of value, management must use the information gained to promote actions and activities, which facilitate the development and utilization of knowledge. Conversely, management must dissuade and improve upon those actions and activities, which hinder learning, sharing, contribution, and participation. The proper structures and incentives can help generate innovation and build knowledge assets.

While knowledge assets are based in the experience and expertise of individuals, managers can provide the environment and conditions to help facilitate developing individual knowledge into organizational expertise. If a learning organization is desired, management must facilitate an environment which celebrates and incents behaviors which lead to learning, sharing, participation, mentoring, and relationship building.

In addition to incentives, structures or processes should be self-rewarding. Displaying the desired behaviors and actions should be beneficial to those participating, and contributors to knowledge creation should get as much if not more benefit as those taking most advantage or benefit from the system. At the same time, the message must be sent that the sharing of knowledge is as valuable and necessary as the demonstration of expertise.

Benefits can be as simple as the ability to use the output and peer recognition, or more significant such as promotions or increased monetary compensation. It is also beneficial to have policies, which dissuade activities such as hoarding of information and knowledge to protect privilege or power. Likewise reduced pay, demotions, and even termination can be effective disincentive. Contributing to knowledge development takes time and effort, and it will not often be done without making this activity part of the daily job. Key to understanding what behaviors and who to reward, as well as how to reward them, is the process of measurement and review. Again, measurement and review is the process whereby knowledge of self and the organization is acquired. If you can envision something, you can measure it; and if you can measure it, you can manage it

Organizations can facilitate the development of knowledge, by managing the review and measurement process. Review and measurement provides the knowledge of self to guide individual and organizational change. Providing focus and guiding change results in an environment in which the development of knowledge occurs. Though it would seem difficult, knowledge development and utilization can be measured. Performance can be measured against objectives to improve compliance. Regular measurement and review provides a benchmark for activities, and allows for the identification of best practices. Additionally, individual performance can be measured and compared over time to monitor if knowledge is being developed and utilized, and attitudes and the environment can be measured and reviewed to ensure they are conducive to the development of a learning organization.

Knowledge is gained during the review and measurement process, but this is not the only value of measurement and review. Management can act on this knowledge to guide behaviors and actions, which leads to continuous improvement and provides for the further development of knowledge workers and increased competitiveness.

TWELVE

The Effects of Time on the
Development of Knowledge

Albert Einstein has been attributed with stating: "Knowledge is experience. Everything else is just information." While the quote may or may not be accurately attributed, the statement seems quite accurate. Reviewing the previous seven elements, which lead to the development of knowledge workers, experience is a common theme.

When employees are hired, one of the most important characteristics employers should look for is previous, relevant, experience. When establishing or influencing the organizational environment, management should try to create a situation in which employees can contribute and enjoy the experience. Leadership provides focus, guidance, and the benefit of another's experience. Training is the process of systematically communicating the experience or knowledge of others. Mentoring is a similar process, though usually less formal and more socially oriented. Processes, as a set of instructions or a method, are a means by which less experienced individuals can achieve similar results as experienced individuals, and at the same time gain experience. Even the measurement and review process provides experience in the form of feedback regarding what works and is successful versus what should be improved or changed.

In a real sense, experience is linked to knowledge, and developing experience, develops knowledge. In working groups, the diverse experience of individuals from different backgrounds, contributes to the pool of tacit and explicit knowledge, available to be drawn upon. Often, the more unique the individual experience, the more valuable is the contribution to the group. Unique and tacit knowledge which resides in the individual is protected from competitors unless these key individuals leave or are hired away. Individuals who possess experiential knowledge can influence the organization in many ways. Statements, suggestions, examples, and mental models all increase the value of possible solutions. Experience allows for the insight and intuition to become inspiration.

Experience is directly linked to knowledge, and the previous seven elements discussed for the development of knowledge, each relate to building on or developing new experience. So what does this have to do with time? Time is the eighth element, which leads to the development of knowledge. Each of the previous elements takes time to perform, accomplish, or get results. For example, training, mentoring, and leadership, are not activities, which happen instantaneously or overnight.

Knowledge is a direct outcome of experiences, reflection, and dialogue, and each of these activities requires that most precious human resource…time. Time is an important element, which must be provided, managed, and allocated for the development of knowledge workers.

Research suggests that deep skills can take at least a decade to develop.[5] Time is required for the development of knowledge workers. A direct example of this was in chapter nine on training and the use of best practice. Research conducted by Gabriel Szulanski, for APQC, indicated best practices could linger unrecognized for years and when recognized, take more

_____

[5] Herbert Simon, 1981, "The Sciences of the Artificial" (Cambridge, MA: MIT Press), p. 106, referenced in Leonard and Sensiper, p. 117.

than two years, on average, before others actively adopted the process.[6] In this scenario, if an individual is involved in an organization for less than two years, it is unlikely they will develop the knowledge associated with the best practice. Conversely, participating in an organization over multiple years should provide for the development of organizational context specific knowledge.

Leaving the organization does not mean the individual will no longer develop knowledge, nor does it mean that knowledge developed elsewhere over the same time period would be either more or less valuable. The amount and quality of the knowledge developed is relative to the quantity and quality of the individuals' experience, which is directly related to the time spent on the elements being discussed.

Experience is fundamental to the development of knowledge, and experience resides in individuals. If participation and involvement is necessary to gain and share experience, management must recognize this and develop organizations and systems, which provide for participation and involvement. This

---

[6] Gabriel Szulanski, 1994, "Intra-Firm Transfer of Best Practices Project," (Houston, TX: American Productivity & Quality Center), referenced in Carla O'Dell and Jackson C. Grayson. Spring 1998. "If Only We Knew What We Know: Identification and Transfer of Internal Best Practices". California Management Review Vol. 40 (3), pp. 155.

requires an investment of energy, capital, and possibly most importantly, time.

Management must spend time, as a resource. Time must be spent selecting the best individuals, time must be spent developing an appropriate environment, time must be spent providing leadership, mentorship, and training; and time must be spent developing processes and reviewing and acting on results. In addition, time must be given as a resource to individuals. Individuals need the resource of time in order to interact, participate, and have the involvement, which is necessary for the development of knowledge. Over time, knowledge will develop. Management can provide the time, and management can reduce the time by providing the other elements.

THIRTEEN

Projects

As organizations and individuals develop and knowledge grows, the implementation of projects allows for continued knowledge development and provides a means for the organization to gain value from workers. In 1997, the Ernst and Young Center for Business Innovation conducted a study, of 431 U.S. and European organizations.[7] This study was an attempt to describe what firms were doing to manage knowledge, what they thought they should be doing, and the barriers they faced.

---

[7] Ruggles, p. 80, quoting a survey-based study with follow-up interviews; full report issued by The Ernst and Young Center for Business Innovation and Business Intelligence as "Executive Perspectives on Knowledge in the Organization," 1997.

In an analysis of the study, Ruggles states one of the ways in which knowledge is managed is by conducting projects intended to improve performance. Based on the study, executives seemed to think that overall performance was poor, in the area of developing and utilizing knowledge (see Figure 2), but they also seemed to believe projects could improve the situation. Figures 3 and 4 show what executives thought was project priorities and the greatest barriers to success of knowledge management projects.

Figure 2: Executive Survey, % of Respondents Who Believe Their Organizations have Good or Excellent Performance

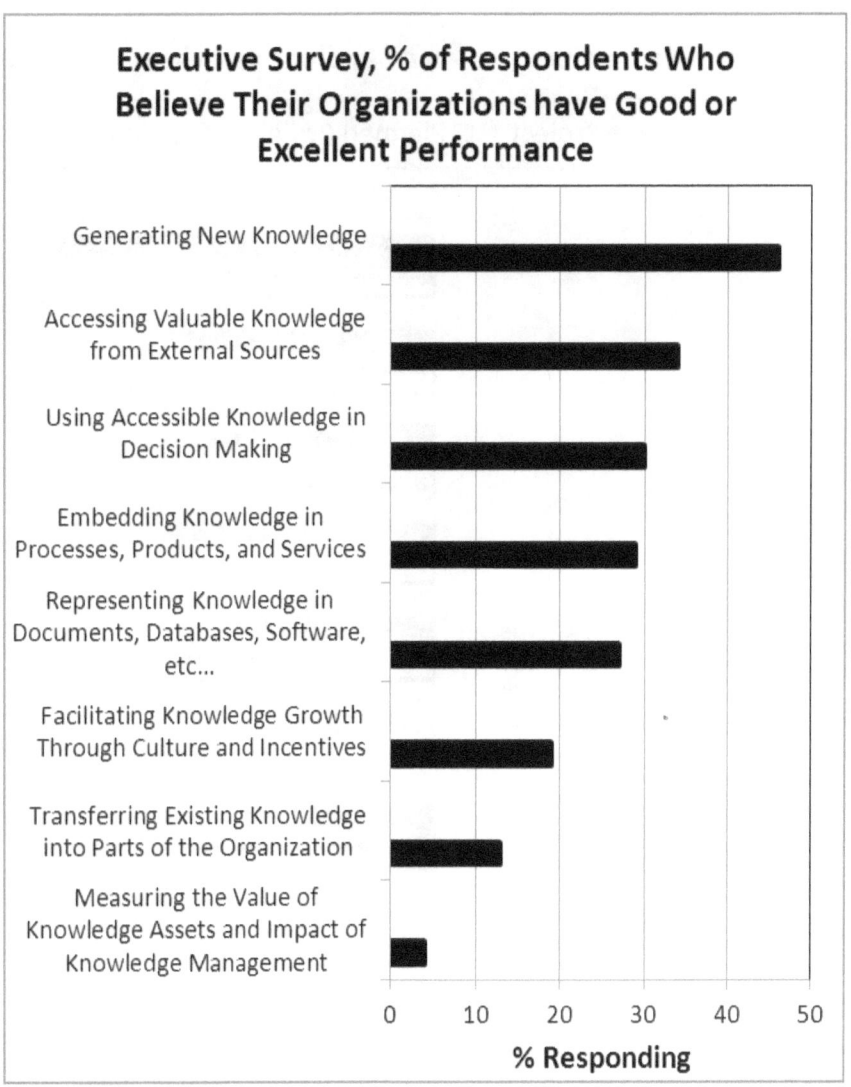

SOURCE: Ruggles, p. 82.

Figure 3: Executive Survey of Project Priorities

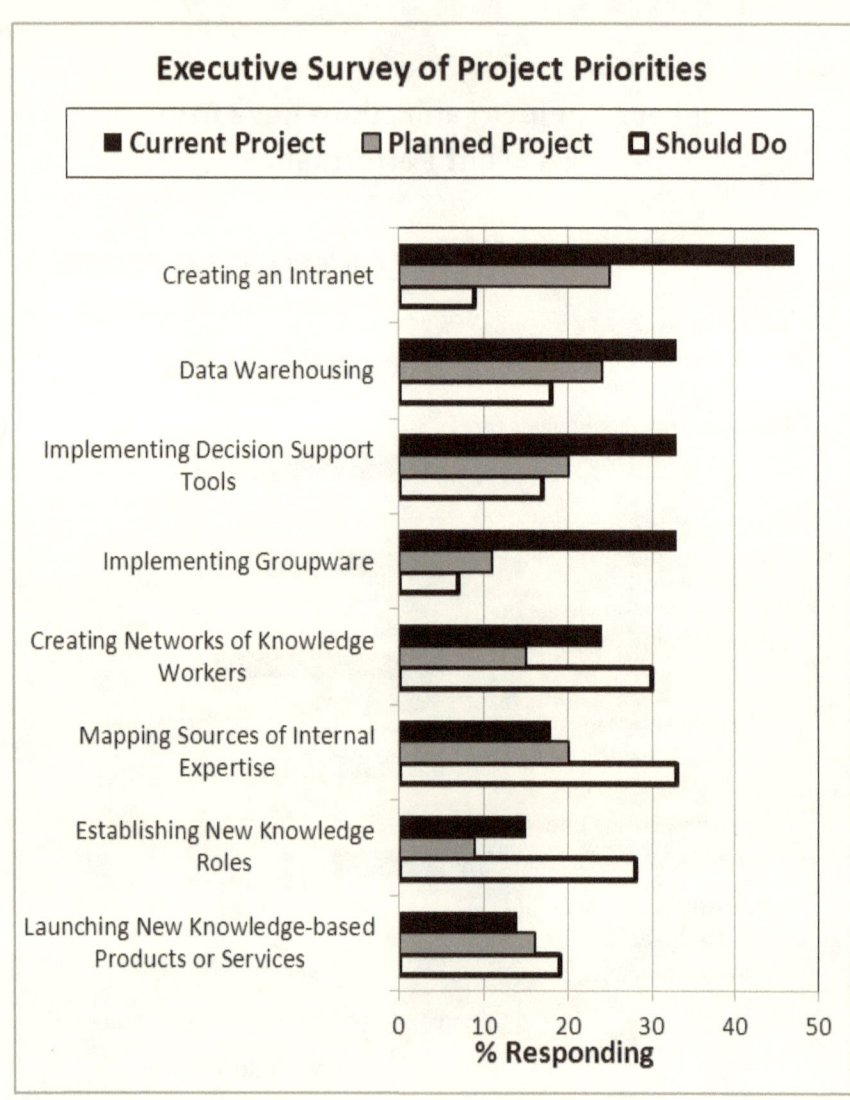

SOURCE: Ruggles, p. 83.

Figure 4: Executive Survey of the Greatest Difficulties to Management

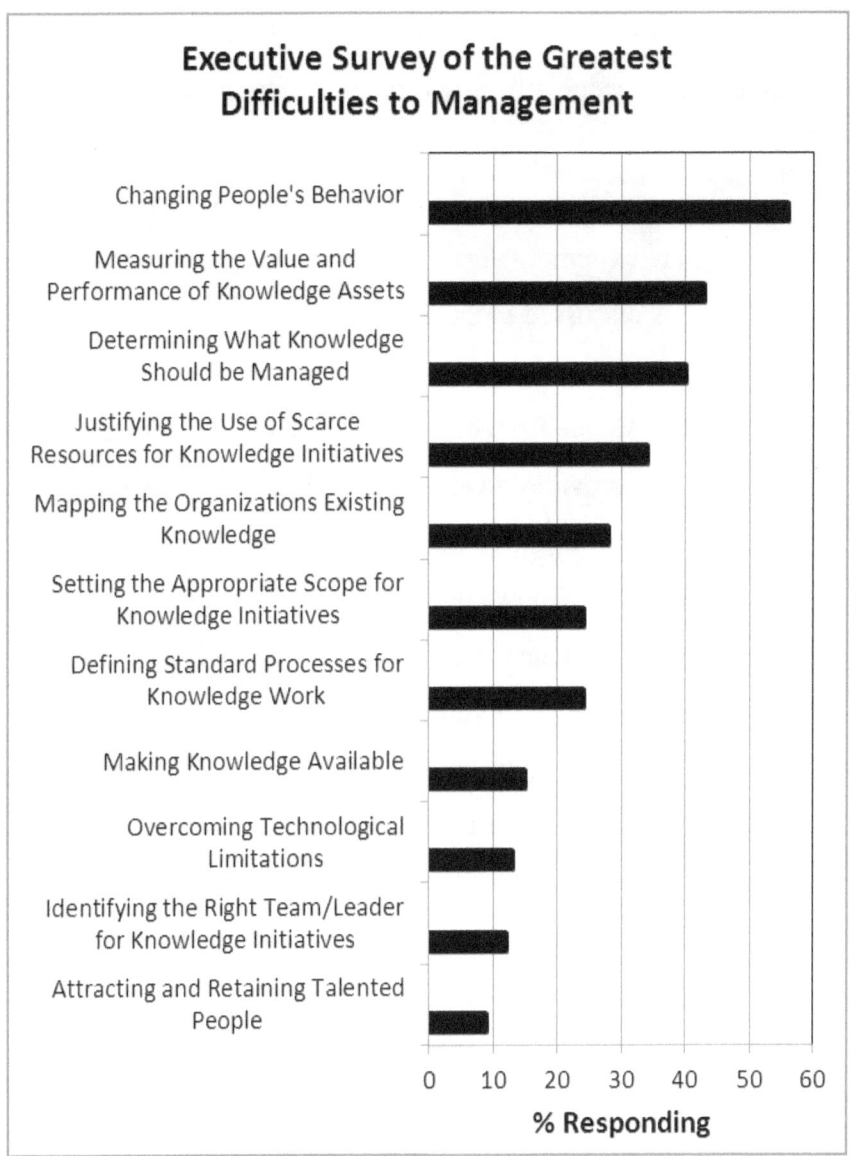

SOURCE: Ruggles, p. 87

Referring to the project priorities identified in the Ernst and Young study, they seem to indicate that most knowledge projects have one of three aims: the codification of knowledge, building a knowledge infrastructure, or developing a culture and focus on knowledge use and development.

Projects designed to promote the codification of knowledge are extremely important. The codification of knowledge, as discussed in the chapters on training and processes, is important to promote the replication and efficient transfer of knowledge from one source to another; codification of knowledge also provides greater accessibility and greater leverage to learning efforts. Codified knowledge improves the possibility of achieving scale in knowledge reuse and growing the business. Projects, which facilitate the codification of knowledge, result in the further development of knowledge and knowledge workers.

Given knowledge is being codified, the next important project aim should be to ensure this knowledge is being utilized. To achieve this end, projects should be used to develop systems and relationships, which promote the utilization of knowledge.

Standard operating procedures, knowledge brokers, electronic repositories, and various types of networks can be implemented to enhance the ability of individuals to access and utilize existing knowledge, and the emphasis should be access and use. Utility, as opposed to power, ownership, and control is the main purpose of the knowledge being created. The four most common projects of this sort, from the Ernst and Young survey, were creating an Intranet, creating knowledge repositories, implementing decision support tools, and implementing GroupWare to support collaboration.

Important to remember, in this modern age, is the fact that I.T. projects, while seemingly the most popular now, will not succeed alone in getting individuals to share knowledge. Leveraging knowledge is actually very hard and is more dependent on community building and relationships than technology, because knowledge, which must be shared, is neither always obvious nor easy to document. In order to build systems and relationships which will increase the exchange of information and the development of knowledge, the systems must provide value and the knowledge or information must have meaning or utility to the user.

The third type of project, which promotes the development of knowledge, is the project designed to develop a culture or focus, within the organization, committed to the use of knowledge for competitive advantage. By developing a culture which values knowledge and the sharing and utilization of knowledge, management can create an environment in which knowledge flows freely and a learning organization develops.

The Ernst and Young study provides an indication of the importance of projects focused on the organizational culture. Changing people's behavior was the greatest difficulty management faced in managing knowledge, and culture was indicated as the greatest obstacle to knowledge transfer. The importance of management focus on developing a culture which values knowledge is evident.

The idea of implementing projects to increase the development and utilization of knowledge and knowledge workers is not new. Approximately two-thirds of the executives in a 1997 Ernst and Young survey believed management could improve on knowledge practices with more deliberate management. The three main areas in which project implementation can help to develop knowledge and knowledge workers are as follows: the implementation of projects to codify knowledge, the implementation of projects to build the systems and relationships, which provide access and utilization of knowledge, and the implementation of projects to develop a culture which values knowledge.

With the proper management commitment, focus, and projects designed to improve the access to and utilization of knowledge within the firm; knowledge can be developed and transferred effectively to meet the strategic objectives of the organization. One of these objectives should be the development of knowledge workers.

Figure 5: Executive Survey of the Greatest Impediment to Knowledge Transfer

SOURCE: Ruggles, p. 88.

FOURTEEN

<u>Relationships</u>

The development of knowledge workers should be a focus of every individual within an organization. Imagine how difficult this process would be, however; if individuals were unable to interact with one another. It seems impossible to provide leadership without communicating with someone. Training, mentoring, and other processes are moot without a knower and a subject to interact. Throughout this work, the importance of interaction and relationships has been discussed, in reference to other knowledge creation elements. Due to its significance, the development of relationships and individual interaction is also a key element to the development of knowledge workers.

Successful organizations must create knowledge and knowledge workers, and one way this is possible is through engagement, interaction, and relationship building. Interaction and the development of individual relationships are paramount to the expansion and development knowledge. Management can better leverage and manage knowledge within the firm by assisting the flow of knowledge through communities. Knowledge is more than processes, documents, and networks; knowledge resides in individuals and the way they think, act and speak. Knowledge is in the stories they tell and the experiences they gain together. People working together can change their thinking and see each other's reasoning as they work on and solve problems together, and all contacts within the community can be vehicles for sharing and developing knowledge, even though most are not intended to be.

In order to leverage knowledge in the community, management must nurture, and develop knowledge communities, which already exist. Since natural learning communities focus on topics that people feel passionate about, focus on relationships and knowledge important to both the business and the people. Management must work to create forums for thinking, as well as, sharing information. Management should help the community decide what and how to share, and the community can keep the right knowledge and information up-to-date and available to community members at the right time to be useful.

The SECI Model demonstrates relationships are also important in practice. The SECI Model portrays knowledge creation as a spiraling process of interactions between explicit and tacit knowledge, and the four steps in the knowledge conversion process (socialization, externalization, internalization, and combination) are premised on the individual interacting with other individuals and groups to develop, exchange, and create new knowledge.

Faced with the importance of building knowledge, creating relationships, and building interaction, what is the role of management? Management must listen to people and understand what they feel is important to the organization. Management must also openly communicate what management feels is important to the organization, including the importance of relationship building and individual interaction to promote knowledge creation.

Dialogue must be encouraged, and relationships nurtured. A shared vision and a shared context will be developed through the communication of what is important to the community as a whole, and through this shared context, the further development of community will occur, increased interaction and improved relationships will emerge. Again, it is important for management to make expectations clear regarding the importance and necessity to pursue knowledge creation through the development and maintenance of productive relationships and interaction.

FIFTEEN

Individuals, Characteristics, and Attitudes

This book presents a number of elements, which provide the basis for the development of knowledge workers. The need for leadership, mentoring, training, and the building of relationships, processes, and open, positive environments to re-name a few. While these elements are important, without individuals to create and participate in these elements, there can be no system or process to develop the knowledge worker. Individuals are attained by the organization, through the hiring process, but attitude comes with an individual, and attitude can have major impacts on the ability of an organization to develop knowledge workers. Additionally, attitude can develop and change over time; who has not heard of the employee with an attitude problem?

Evaluating the importance of the individual, it is not surprising that documenting procedures, linking people electronically, or creating web sites is often not enough. The challenge to the organization is to get people to think together. To improve upon or build upon the ideas they have as individuals, in order to generate new, shared, knowledge and context. Individuals working together can share insights they didn't even realize they had until another perspective is applied. Rather than identifying a knowledge creation system in the form of information needs and tools, management should identify the community of individuals who care about a topic, and then enhance their ability to think together, stay in touch with each other, share ideas with each other, and connect with other communities. Focusing on the people who use knowledge, a significant aspect is their attitude, perspective and character.

The hiring process, performed well, can provide the best available resource for the organization. This resource however must be fully developed and utilized to provide maximum competitive value, and this means the emotional and psychological aspects of the employee must be considered and developed.

One of the most important characteristics or attitudes, which must be developed, is a sense of purpose. Leadership, vision, and goals can help to develop a sense of purpose in individuals, but ultimately the individual must demonstrate commitment to the vision and goals. For individuals who possess a sense of purpose, a vision is a realistic objective, and not just a good idea. When individuals demonstrate purpose, they not only demonstrate commitment to goals, but they demonstrate an understanding of current reality and the flexibility or desire to change.

Developing a sense of purpose can also be associated with developing a sense of urgency. The old saying, something worth doing, is worth doing well, can be modified to if something is worth doing, it is worth doing in a timely fashion. When individuals possess a sense of purpose coupled with a sense of urgency, motivation to complete the task would seemingly be high. If the task is to increase knowledge and develop knowledge workers for organizational success, developing a sense of purpose and urgency within individuals would seemingly provide the motivation or "right attitude" to complete the task.

A second personal characteristic or attitude, which should be developed, is the desire or willingness to participate. Whether referring to developing and maintaining relationships, or merely interacting with others, participation is imperative to the acquisition and sharing of information and knowledge, and it is the ongoing acquisition and sharing of knowledge which directly leads to the development of knowledge workers.

Knowledge is acquired through one's own experience or reflections on the experiences of others. To participate and get involved allows the individual to transcend their own limited perspective. Individuals, who get involved, participate, collaborate, and share knowledge, contribute to the development of knowledge and knowledge workers, therefore an attitude of sharing and participation must be developed.

The third attitude that should be developed is care. Care is defined as serious attention, a feeling of concern and interest. Management should seek individuals who demonstrate aspects of care in their work, in their relationships, and in their personal growth. The process of individual growth is the basis for the development of knowledge workers, and developing an attitude of care for individuals as well as the organization, provides a method for individual and organizational growth and learning.

Care can also be associated with ownership, commitment, and support. In many ways individuals make both a physical and emotional investment, when they participate in an organization. This investment can be evaluated, and the level of participation can imply the amount of individual care, and when care exists, there is a commitment to growth and development.

In order to develop knowledge workers, individuals must care for, value, and commit to the development of knowledge workers. An organization's commitment to, and capacity for learning is no greater than that of its members. The role of management should be to develop care and commitment from individuals. In many cases, individuals start at a workplace with great intentions; they are bright, energetic, and educated. Within a few years, a small subset are on the fast-track, and the rest are taking up space and collecting a check, doing what is expected to get by. They lose the commitment and the excitement with which they started their careers. In order to prevent this situation, these employees must be engaged to take ownership, increase commitment and support, and lastly to have care for the organization as well as personal growth. Ultimately, to actualize knowledge development, individuals and organizations must be committed to learning, and care for each other and the learning process.

In addition to having purpose, being participative, and caring; individuals should develop other attitudes or characteristics such as thoughtfulness, trust, initiative, and the willingness to learn. The level at which these characteristics exist within the individual, is a direct influence on the attitude and behavior of the individual. This in turn is a direct influence on the ability of the individual to develop and assist others in becoming knowledge workers.

In simple terms, having or developing individuals with the aforementioned character or attitudes could be described as having grown-ups in the workplace. Whether you call it personal mastery, Meta-knowledge, or emotional IQ; however it is described, the character and attitude of individual employee's directly impacts the ability to develop knowledge and knowledge workers.

The active force in any aspect of business is the individual. The individual having his own mind and will behaves and acts as he chooses. Management can develop a sense of purpose, participation, and care in the individual through the employment relationship. Providing a means for support of one-self and family can be a great motivator. Alternatively, the employment relationship can present the opportunity to be part of something far greater than one-self. Individuals either have a need to commit, care, and have purpose; or they desire to. This can be managed.

Providing responsibility, autonomy, ownership, incentives, and consequences promotes initiative to act with purpose, participation, commitment to, and care for the organization. Individual attitudes and motivation come from within; but self-regulation, care, character, attitude, whatever it is called, can be elicited by management through the creation of the environment and consistent communication of the desired message. If the message communicates "develop knowledge, a learning organization, and knowledge workers", this should in all likelihood be the result.

SIXTEEN

The Knowledge to Action Gap

An old medical joke goes like this: Internists know everything and do nothing; surgeons know nothing and do everything; pathologists know everything and do everything -- but too late. The basis of this humor is the gap that exists between knowledge and action. All the knowledge the pathologist possesses is meaningless to the patient expired on the table.

In everyday situations, at companies around the world, we can only imagine the number of cases where employees have access to valuable information and possess the knowledge to do a job better, but lack the authority or ability to act. Knowledge is not power; the ability to act with knowledge is power. All of the elements discussed, which lead to the development of knowledge and knowledge workers, are each irrelevant without the ability or motivation to act. Knowledge is about changing data and information into decisions and action. This is the vital role performed by human intervention. Knowledge without purpose is wasted, and knowing alone is insufficient; human action must occur to realize the benefits and potential of knowledge and knowledge workers. This action will only occur through self-initiative, leadership, or directive.

Action itself in my viewpoint is more important than planning or knowing. Through action, there exists an opportunity for learning, experience is gained, and the environment is established. Knowing comes from doing, teaching, and experimenting. Individuals learn from what works, from what does not work, and from thinking about what has been done. Additionally, reviewing what has been done and again acting to change and improve the existing environment is the basis for continuous improvement and the further development of knowledge.

Acting on what is known can include accessing valuable knowledge from internal and external sources, using knowledge in decision making, embedding knowledge in processes, projects, and services, representing or codifying knowledge in documents, databases, and software. Acting on knowledge can include facilitating knowledge growth through culture and incentives, transferring knowledge throughout the organization, and measuring the impacts and results based on the implementation of knowledge. Each of these activities increases the level of knowledge in an organization, and each of these activities requires individual action. Acting on knowledge, not only to develop it, but also to utilize the knowledge, provides competitive advantage.

Each year, billions of dollars are spent on management consultants by organizations seeking advice. In many cases the advice is not implemented, or not followed up on in the manner conceived. In some cases, I am sure this exercise is conducted multiple times providing the same recommendations from multiple sources and still the recommendations are rejected. Paying for perspective and knowledge and not implementing it would seem to be a waste. Similarly, companies can oftentimes get the same recommendations from knowledgeable internal employees, and yet not realize the validity or take action, until an external consultant tells them the same think.

This gap between knowledge and action is not unique to the consulting business. Surely, most everyone is aware of examples in their own life and workplace, where ideas and plans have been developed, discussed, documented, and even directed to be employed, and yet action has not been taken. In this type of situation, how can management bridge the knowledge to action gap?

Closing the knowledge to action gap, or resolving this performance paradox, contributes to learning and facilitates greater competitiveness. Management can work towards closing the gap in a number of ways. One important practice is to help employees know why to act, before how. By identifying an objective and a strategy, management facilitates employees developing the necessary knowledge to meet the objective and they provide the motive for action.

Another method for reducing the knowledge to action gap is to build existing knowledge into products, processes, and systems. By linking knowledge to its use in a process for example, individuals act with knowledge each time they follow or complete the process. Use of such products, processes, and systems not only results in repetitive experiential learning, but also facilitates an environment in which action is expected (the completion of a process or the use of a product or system for example).

Repeating an often-stated mantra, management must create an environment and establish a norm in which building knowledge, transferring knowledge, and acting on knowledge to meet goals and objectives is the main driver of the organization. Management must effectively communicate that developing knowledge and acting on knowledge is valued and important to the success of the individual and the organization. A manager must understand his job is not to know everything and decide everything, but rather to create an environment in which there are people who both know and take action. Leaders must create environments, reinforce norms, and set expectations through their actions and not just their words.

Closing the knowledge to action gap is more than just providing empowerment and delegation, it also requires giving direction, assigning responsibility, and providing accountability. For actions to occur, people either want to act, or they must act. Individuals want to act when they find participation rewarding, easy, and fun. Often activities which provide personal or organizational, growth and gain, require time, effort, and work; individuals may not often recognize the reward. In these situations, assigning responsibility and accountability is often the only way to precipitate action. When distractions become more important than performance, valuable employees need to be set straight or management may have to risk losing them.

SEVENTEEN

<u>Retain What You Create</u>

Twelve elements, which lead to the development of knowledge workers, have been presented. These elements represent activities, such as project implementation and the codification of knowledge. These elements represent concepts; such as vision, commitment, and the importance of attitudes. These elements also represent conditions, as they relate to relationships and the environment. Effectively developing each of these elements requires time, energy, capital, and the focus of management.

When an organization commits time, energy, and capital to developing a resource or asset, the organization should take appropriate measures to guard against loss of the asset and ensure a return on investment. The value of knowledge workers, more explicitly, workers whose knowledge is specific to your organization or field can be significant if not impossible to replace. Therefore, employee retention is considered to be the last of the elements presented in this work, necessary for the development of knowledge workers to increase the competitiveness of organizations.

Looking only at the cost of employee turnover; Deloitte & Touche estimated in 1999, recruitment and training to replace the average non professional was $12,000, and this cost went to $35,000 per new professional employee.[8] The Families and Work Institute estimates the cost at 75% and 150% of the first year's salary for non-managers and managers respectively.[9] Data from the 1999 Emerging Workforce Study places the cost of losing a typical employee at $50,000.[10] While in the IT field, The Gartner Group estimates turnover, including training, recruitment, interviews, replacement salary, and lost productivity during the learning curve, culminate in costs of approximately $100,000 per

---

[8] "Employee Recruitment and Retention: Strategies for Finding and Keeping Superior Talent." 1999. *Sample Issue ER909*. Lawrence Ragan Communications, Inc. Chicago, IL. p. 11.

[9] Ibid, p. 11.

[10] Jennifer Reingold. 1 March 1999. "Why Your Workers Might Jump Ship." *Business Week*, (3618), p. 8.

employee.[11] While the estimates vary, and have likely increased over the past decade; it is evident the cost of losing valuable employees is significant.

In addition to the costs related to replacing employees, there are costs associated with the loss of valuable employees. In a recent survey of managers and employees, more than 60% of those surveyed agreed that turnover among top performers makes it more difficult for the organization to reach its goals. Additionally, 47% of supervisors and 38% of workers said that their organizations had suffered financial loss when key personnel chose to work elsewhere.[12]

Similar studies by Frederick Reichheld, indicate revolving door defections can have a clearly defined impact on profits. Data from 1996 found 5% swings in retention rates resulted in 25% to 100% changes in earnings: decreased retention resulted in decreased earnings, and increased retention resulted in improved earnings.[13] Clearly, losing knowledgeable workers can have a big

---

[11] Scott Maddern, 1 February 2000, "High-tech Brain Drain: Outsourcing May Help When You're Faced With A Shortage of IT Personnel.," *America's Network* Vol. 104 (2), p. 70.

[12] Kepner-Tregoe, Inc., "Avoiding the brain drain: What companies are doing to lock in their talent," a survey conducted by, Kepner-Tregoe, Inc. Princeton, NJ, referenced in Employee Recruitment and Retention, p. 9.

[13] Frederick Reichheld, 2001, *Loyalty Rules!: How Today's Leaders Build Lasting Relationships,* (Harvard University Press), quoted in Mara Der Hovanesian, 13 August 2001, "When Loyalty Erodes, So Do Profits," *Business Week*, (3745), p. 8.

impact on organizations competitiveness, and if the employee just lost is the individual who would have taught, trained, or mentored your new employees, the ability to maintain and develop a learning organization has just been diminished.

Developing a system and management practice in which the selection, development, and retention of the employee resource is a main focus, provides a situation where the companies best able to develop knowledge workers will be able to acquire the cream of the crop, achieve greater results while they are employed, and keep employees a little bit longer than the competition.

While the costs of turnover and the importance of employee retention are obviously demonstrated, blindly pursuing the retention of all employees is not the solution. Organizations and managers must actively work to develop employees and guide them to productive action. Management must also identify those individuals who either lack the capacity, the capability, or the commitment to produce desirable results and either remove these employees or re-deploy the asset.

Selective retention based on the recognition of the value of the human resource is not a new idea; people are fired or let go from company's everyday. An important message to convey is the importance of recognizing the significance and the impacts of this management practice, not only for the benefit of eliminating poor performance, but also for the opportunity it presents to replace low performance with high performance and learning. This concept is the basis for past actions of CEO's such as Jack Welch of GE and Jacques Nasser of Ford. It is also a belief held by others.

Once valued employees have been identified, what can be done to improve retention? Evaluation of the reasons why employees leave, leads to the conclusion there is no single reason. Instead, there are a variety of reasons surrounding compensation, benefits, and cognitive or emotional issues.

To address these issues, organizations can improve or provide competitive pay, increased benefits, stock options, profit sharing, tuition assistance, casual dress codes, increased training, flexible hours, and a variety of other perks to name a few. Improved communications, mentorship, autonomy, responsibility, opportunity, job security, and direction are less clear-cut or easily valued, yet often desired compensation. Perhaps more important are the psychological aspects of employee participation, belonging, ownership, trust, camaraderie, pride, and freedom.

Each of the aforementioned items and the levels at which they exist impact the ability of management and the organization to retain valuable employees. The opportunity or potential of a job, is often more important to retention than the money or perks. Additionally, different benefits are valued differently, depending on the age and sex of the employee. Management should be aware of individual employees and their needs, in order to be able to understand their values and issues important specifically to their retention. By doing so, organizations retain valuable services, loyalty, and the ability to further develop employee knowledge.

Ability, values, and life interests are the three main drivers of human feelings and behaviors regarding employment. Ability is important to productive engagement. Without the necessary ability most people will not stay in a particular work environment. Similarly, people rarely take jobs, which do not match their values. If individuals value power and influence, they will not likely remain in a job, which has none. Lastly, and most important, it is possible to be good at a job and have the ability, and at the same time like the rewards received from the job, but without interest in the work itself, long-term fulfillment is not probable. Therefore, life interest is a key aspect to long-term retention.

Once again, effectively managing retention issues means having effective managers. Most factors, which influence employee satisfaction and retention, are in the direct control of the immediate supervisor. Everything from the selection process to the ongoing support and development of the employee is either a result of direct management action or indirect management influence. In many cases, the individual manager can not change the benefit package. However, there are many other opportunities each day for management to have a positive impact on the beliefs, attitudes, and activities of individual employee.

People want to participate in activities in which they have life interest. People want to belong, and people want to matter and make a difference. Management is the vehicle by which organizations match people with opportunities. Effective management of the employee retention issue allows individuals to meet their economic, social, and psychological needs while at the same time providing a valuable resource for the organization and contributing to the development of knowledge workers for competitive success.

138

EIGHTEEN

<u>Management, the Overall</u>

<u>Concept</u>

The thirteen elements, which lead to the creation or development of knowledge workers, are directly impacted by one overall concept. Effective management ties all of the elements together to allow organizations to develop knowledge workers to improve competitive success.

Developing individuals into knowledge workers begins with the hiring process. Getting the right people is what the hiring process is all about. The process of creating knowledge workers to improve organizational success is directly related to the ability of management to acquire individuals with the capacity to become knowledge workers. Since management is the most important position within the organization when considering the selection of the most qualified individual, it is imperative that management makes the hiring process an area of focus, specifically with the creation of knowledge workers in mind.

Once valuable employees are acquired, the culture, which develops, can become one of the main impediments to knowledge transfer. Deliberate management can indeed overcome this obstacle as well. While there can be no single best method, structure, or organizational design to develop knowledge workers, management can guide the organizational environment to create a learning organization. By providing focus, direction, and time; by encouraging freedom, responsibility, and the sharing of information and ideas; and through supporting and nurturing individuals, learning is increased.

Leadership, vision, and goals have a significant impact on the development of knowledge workers. Therefore, managing these items increases the likelihood of success in having knowledge workers develop. Managers must demonstrate they value individual leadership; natural leaders should be sought, promoted, and supported. Management must continuously communicate the message that knowledge, learning, and development are valued and they are being evaluated.

Additionally, managers can demonstrate leadership by communicating a vision of a learning organization and setting goals, which are compatible with developing knowledge workers.

Management must take an active role in facilitating the development of individuals through training. As mentioned earlier, people learn what they need to learn; and management must provide guidance as to what is needed. People learn best when they have a genuine sense of responsibility for their actions; because of this, management must develop an environment in which individuals feel accountable for the success of their training and learning process. Additionally, management must facilitate the resources and nurture the relationships, which are required to maximize the training environment.

Management can help to guide the training process in several ways. Actively scanning the environment for changes can identify future training needs. Instituting performance benchmarking to continually monitor historical performance can help identify areas where remedial or additional training may be required. By implementing continuous improvement processes, new methods and procedures can be developed and implemented into training. As mentioned earlier, the sharing of best practices can be stressed to improve the transfer rate within the organization. Each of these activities is directly impacted by the involvement of management.

Management can establish the commitment to learning and the importance of training, through the role of reward and punishment. If a manager values the individual who continues to learn, and an environment of sharing information and developing knowledge is desired, then a system must be set up to encourage, enable, and reward those behaviors which achieve this goal and discourage those behaviors which are counter-productive.

Management can facilitate knowledge development through mentoring programs, but first they must recognize mentoring relationships have value, measure them, reward them, and act on developing these relationships. If individuals are rewarded for hoarding knowledge, they will do so. If expertise is rewarded but mentoring is not, people will not surrender power. Policies, which increase the number and quality of mentoring relationships, must be pursued.

While mentorship itself is hard to measure, the skills gained through mentoring can be assessed. Individuals can be judged by their performance, which is an indicator of the successfulness of the mentoring relationship. Management can then act on the performance information to work to improve the mentoring programs. Ultimately, management must come to realize mentors and mentorship needs to be nurtured, supported, enhanced, and cared for.

Management can facilitate the development of knowledge workers through processes. In order to achieve the most benefit from process knowledge, management must manage, develop, and continuously improve the processes of the organization. Management must develop processes to facilitate the codification, indexing, and distribution of knowledge and management must institute processes and routines, which facilitate the development of relationships, important to the sharing of knowledge, both within and outside the organization.

In order to accomplish this task and ensure processes are developed and followed, people need incentives to participate. Management needs to develop a system, which encourages individuals to follow existing processes, continuously improve these processes, and document and share process information. The ability to follow and improve process, and the level and quality of employee contribution to process documentation are all subject to review and appraisal. The ability to demonstrate the establishment of personal relationships for the direct sharing of knowledge, while more difficult to measure, is also subject to review when it comes time for annual compensation. If management does not make expectations clear, and reward desired behaviors, individuals will not likely go out of their way to develop and improve processes on their own.

If people do not develop and improve processes currently; and if process knowledge is not being shared today; then codification and technology solutions will not likely help. Individuals must understand the importance and significance of process knowledge and management must provide leadership and support. Management is important to communicate, demonstrate, and facilitate the understanding of the importance of processes, in order to achieve the desired outcome, the development of knowledge workers and improved competitiveness.

Organizations can facilitate the development of knowledge, by managing the review and measurement process. Review and measurement provides the knowledge of self to guide individual and organizational change. Providing focus and guiding change results in an environment in which the development of knowledge occurs. Though it would seem difficult, knowledge development and utilization can be measured. Performance can be measured to improve compliance, to benchmark activities, and develop best practices. Additionally, performance can be measured to monitor if knowledge is being developed and utilized, and attitudes and the environment can be measured and reviewed to ensure they are conducive to the development of a learning organization.

Knowledge is gained during the review and measurement process, but this is not the only value of measurement and review. Management can act on this knowledge to guide behaviors and actions, which lead to the further development of knowledge workers and increased competitiveness.

Experience is fundamental to the development of knowledge, and experience resides in individuals. If participation and involvement is necessary to gain and share experience, management must recognize this and develop the organizations and systems, which provide for participation and involvement. This requires an investment of energy, capital, and possibly most importantly, time.

Management must utilize the resource of time effectively. Time must be spent selecting the best individuals, time must be spent developing an appropriate environment, time must be spent providing leadership, mentorship, and training, and time must be spent developing processes and reviewing and acting on results. In addition, time must be given as a resource to individuals. Individuals need the resource of time in order to interact, participate, and have the involvement, which is necessary for the development of knowledge. Over time, knowledge will develop.

Management can provide the time, and management can reduce the amount time required, by providing the other elements mentioned.

Through the implementation of projects, management can increase the utilization of knowledge and the development of knowledge workers. The three main areas in which project implementation can help to develop knowledge and knowledge workers are as follows: the implementation of projects to codify knowledge, the implementation of projects to build the systems and relationships, which provide access and utilization of knowledge, and the implementation of projects to develop a culture which values knowledge.

With the proper management commitment and focus, and projects designed to improve the access to and utilization of knowledge within the firm; knowledge can be developed and transferred effectively to meet the strategic objectives of the organization. One of these objectives should be the development of knowledge workers.

Faced with the importance of building knowledge-creating relationships and increasing interaction, management must listen to people and understand what they feel is important to the organization. Management must also openly communicate what management views as important to the organization, which

146

should include the importance of relationship building and individual interaction to promote knowledge creation.

Dialogue must be encouraged and relationships nurtured. A shared vision and a shared context will be developed through the communication of what is important to the community as a whole; and through this shared context, the further development of community will occur. Increased interaction and improved relationships will emerge. Again, it is important for management to make expectations clear regarding the importance and necessity to pursue knowledge creation through the development and maintenance of productive relationships and interaction.

The active force in any aspect of business is the individual; and the individual having his own mind and will, behaves and acts as he chooses. Management must develop a sense of purpose, participation, and care in the individual through the employment relationship. Providing a means for support of one-self and family can be a great motivator. Alternatively, the employment relationship can present the opportunity to be part of something far greater than one-self. Individuals either have a need to commit, care, and have purpose; or they desire to. This can be managed.

Providing responsibility, autonomy, ownership, incentives, and consequences promotes initiative to act with purpose, participation, commitment to, and care for the organization. Individual attitudes and motivation come from within; but management through the creation of the environment and consistent communication of the desired message can elicit self-regulation, care, character, and attitude. If the message is "develop knowledge, a learning organization, and knowledge workers," This should in all likelihood be the result.

Management can also develop knowledge workers by closing the knowledge to action gap. Resolving the *performance paradox* contributes to learning and facilitates greater competitiveness. Management can work towards closing the gap in a number of ways. One important practice is to help employees know why to act, before how. By identifying an objective and a strategy, management facilitates employees developing the necessary knowledge to meet the objective and they provide the motive for action.

Another method for reducing the knowledge to action gap is to build existing knowledge into products, processes, and systems. By linking knowledge to its use in a process for example, individuals act with knowledge each time they follow or complete the process. Use of such products, processes, and systems not only results in repetitive experiential learning, but also facilitates an environment in which action is expected.

Closing the knowledge to action gap is more than just providing empowerment and delegation, it also requires giving direction, assigning responsibility, and providing accountability. For actions to occur, people either want to act, or they must act. Individuals want to act when they find participation rewarding, easy, and fun. Often activities which provide personal or organizational growth and gain require time, effort, and work; individuals may not often recognize the reward. In these situations, assigning responsibility and accountability is often the only way to precipitate action.

Lastly, effective management recognizes the importance of the retention of valuable employee resources. Effectively managing retention issues means having effective managers. Most factors, which influence employee satisfaction and retention, are in the direct control of the immediate supervisor. Everything from the selection process to the ongoing support and development of the employee is either a result of direct management action or indirect management influence. While not all issues can be changed by the individual manager; there are many opportunities each day for management to have a positive impact on the beliefs, attitudes, and activities of individual employees.

People want to participate in activities in which they have life interest. People want to belong, and people want to matter and make a difference. Management is the vehicle by which organizations match people with opportunities. Effective management of the employee retention issue allows individuals to meet their economic, social, and psychological needs while at the same time providing a valuable resource for the organization and contributing to the development of knowledge workers for competitive success.

Once again, repeating an often-stated mantra, management must create an environment and establish a norm in which building, transferring, and acting on knowledge to meet goals and objectives is the main driver of the organization. Management must effectively communicate, through actions and words, that developing and acting on knowledge is valued and important to the success of the individual and the organization. Managers must recognize they are responsible to provide the physical and social structure, systems, and relationships, which develop knowledge. Lastly, management must link the use and development of knowledge and knowledge workers to the strategy of the organization.

NINETEEN

<u>Conclusion</u>

Utilizing knowledge to compete more effectively has definite economic and competitive value. Similarly, there is measurable cost or lost value, when an organization losses knowledge or knowledge workers. More difficult to assuage is the value of existing or potential knowledge prior to utilization or loss.

Knowledge, like electricity, can not be seen directly, but only through effects. While it can not be seen, it can be stored, monitored, and changed. Unlike most resources, rather than being non-renewable and exhibiting decreasing returns, knowledge often increases in value the more it is utilized and is essentially self reproducing. These characteristics must be taken into account to develop a measure of value. Knowledge for the most part, seems to have value only when used, and knowledge development will not likely occur until organizations understand what real value knowledge and knowledge workers represent.

There is no specific formula for developing knowledge workers, to do so is more of an art form. Since individuals hold knowledge, managing knowledge development implies managing the development of individuals. What is proposed is the role of management combined with the existence of specific elements, which contribute to knowledge development. This work is not meant to detail how to manage, but to stress that organizations and individuals must manage; this is an obligation not only to share holders, but to employees and managers themselves. While various methods may be employed for the implementation of some or all of these elements; simply recognizing the concept and taking any action at all should provide improvement over the status quo, but as always, the choice to act is within each individual.

More people, more technology, more information, and more access to all of these results in an environment that is rapidly changing; but with the right people in the right positions, organizations can function and excel in this environment. People are the key to organizational success. The characteristics of competency, self initiative, cooperation, adaptability, quality focus, entreprenuerialism, vision, and the support of organizational goals all result in increased competitiveness.

In order to maximize the potential of human resources in an organization, managers should give considerable thought and attention to matters of selection, training, and leadership of the people they employ. By selecting individuals who possess the previously mentioned attributes or by imparting these attributes through training and leadership; managers can increase the likelihood of success in today's environment.

The best management, the newest tools, the latest technology, and the best processes play an important role, but the capabilities that create a competitive advantage come from people, their skill, problem solving ability, flexibility, motivation, and capacity to learn and apply what they know. Developing their potential is the critical factor in significantly improving performance.

Bibliography

Der Hovanesian, Mara. 31 August 2001. "When Loyalty Erodes, So Do Profits." *Business Week,* (3745), p. 8.

Ditka, Mike. 1995. "Many People One Goal." *Game Plans for Success* (NFL Properties Inc.) .

"Employee Recruitment and Retention: Strategies for Finding and Keeping Superior Talent." 1999. *Sample Issue ER909.* Lawrence Ragan Communications, Inc. Chicago, IL. pp. 1-12.

Farkas, Charles and Suzy Wetlaufer. May-June 1996. "The Ways Chief Executive Officers Lead." *Harvard Business Review* Vol. 74 (3), pp. 110-122.

Kepner-Tregoe, Inc., "Avoiding the brain drain: What companies are doing to lock in their talent," a survey conducted by, Kepner-Tregoe, Inc. Princeton, NJ,

Leonard, Dorothy and Sylvia Sensiper. Spring 1998. "The Role of Tacit Knowledge in Group Innovation." *California Management Review* Vol. 40 (3), pp. 112-132.

Maddern, Scott. February 1999. "High-tech Brain Drain: Outsourcing May Help When You're Faced With A Shortage of IT Personnel." *America's Network* Vol. 104 (2), pp. 70-72.

Nonaka, Ikujiro and Noboru Konno. Spring 1998. "The Concept of "Ba": Building a Foundation for Knowledge Creation." *California Management Review* Vol. 40 (3), pp. 40-41.

O'Dell, Carla and Jackson C. Grayson. Spring 1998. "If Only We Knew What We Know: Identification and Transfer of Internal Best Practices." *California Management Review* Vol. 40 (3), pp. 154-174.

Reingold, Jennifer. 1 March 1999. "Why Your Workers Might Jump Ship." *Business Week*, (3618), p. 8.

Ruggles, Rudy. Spring 1998. "The State of the Notion: Knowledge Management in Practice." *California Management Review* Vol. 40 (3), pp. 80-89.

Simon, Herbert. 1981, The Sciences of the Artificial (*Cambridge, MA: MIT Press*), p. 106.

Gabriel Szulanski, 1994, "Intra-Firm Transfer of Best Practices Project," (*Houston, TX: American Productivity & Quality Center*),

www.ingramcontent.com/pod-product-compliance
Lightning Source LLC
Chambersburg PA
CBHW032019170526
45157CB00002B/770